GARDENS
~ OF THE ~
SPIRIT

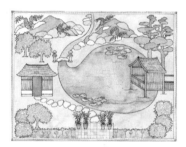

GARDENS

~ OF THE ~

SPIRIT

CREATE YOUR OWN
SACRED SPACES

RONI JAY

Sterling Publishing Co., Inc.
New York

Library of Congress
Cataloging-in-Publication Data Available

Published in 1998 by Sterling Publishing Company, Inc.
387 Park Avenue South, New York, N.Y. 10016

Originally published in Great Britain in 1998 by
GODSFIELD PRESS

Picture research by *Jan Croot*
Illustrations by *Lorraine Harrison*

Distributed in Canada by Sterling Publishing
c/o Canadian Manda Group, One Atlantic Avenue. Suite 105
Toronto, Ontario, Canada M6K 3E7

Printed and bound in Singapore

ISBN 0-8069-0725-8

CONTENTS

A PIECE OF HEAVEN

What exactly is it about gardens that has captured people's imaginations for so long? The garden has always meant the same thing to every culture — it is the representation of Paradise on Earth. It is our opportunity to own a little bit of Heaven here and now. Even the word "Paradise" comes from the Persian word for a garden.

Around 4,000 years ago, in China, the first gardens were made. Within a few hundred years, the people of the Mediterranean and Near East began to create gardens for themselves as well. Since then, just about every culture that survives above a subsistence level has included gardening among its pleasures. And those of us who have our own gardens, whether it is a windowbox or several acres, know the satisfaction of creating a garden.

Even in the practical, scientific world of the twentieth century, we still need gardens — perhaps now more than ever. We may read books and magazine articles that tell us about the pH of the soil, or how to pot on our houseplants, or how to get the maximum yield from our raspberry canes. But we all know, deep down, that is not what it's all about. It is about taming a small piece of nature to create our own Paradise. And since we are all different, our ideas of Heaven are different — so our own garden is never quite the same as anyone else's.

It's not only the pleasure of sitting or walking in a garden that explains its appeal. Every aspect of creating your own Heaven has its attraction. There is something deep inside us that needs to create perfection in order to balance those parts of our life that are imperfect. Whether you are planting up a windowbox or designing a five-acre plot, it is an opportunity to let your imagination run free. A garden is a partnership with nature, and cultures through the ages have demonstrated a different attitude to this relationship. Some seek to imitate nature, some to control it — the art of bonsai is probably the clearest example of this — and others to work alongside it in a garden that is close to being wild. But no garden will thrive unless the gardener respects these natural forces. Whichever your preferred style, gardening brings you closer to nature, and therefore closer to your own god.

The process of creating and maintaining a garden also has a deeply spiritual side to it. Attaining the perfect garden entails constant hard work just as attaining Heaven does. A garden needs constant maintenance, as does our relationship with whatever god or gods we worship. Yet, as every keen gardener knows, this is not a chore but part of the inspiration of a garden — that we must work constantly at our partnership with nature.

LEFT: Gardens have always been an inspiration for artists: The Herb Garden After Harvest (detail), by the contemporary artist, Timothy Easton.

The plants we grow also represent our own spirituality. They will not thrive unless we nurture them with water, food, and the warmth and light of the sun. In the same way we must nurture ourselves with the water of the spirit, the food of knowledge, and the light and warmth of love.

Many of the tasks we have to carry out in the garden, such as weeding and pruning, are a form of meditation. They have the same effect of removing stress and focusing or emptying the mind. The Zen monks understood this so well that they even created meditation rituals around the maintenance of their gardens.

The Spiritual Elements of a Garden

These elements of gardening have appealed to gardeners and garden designers around the world. Every culture has had features that were especially important because of their own view of Heaven. In many cultures, water is seen as one of the most important ingredients of life and, usually, of the story of Creation itself. It is one of the four Western elements, and one of the five elements of the Eastern world. Without it we would die, and the crops would fail to grow.

Since water is so important on Earth, it must surely be important in Heaven. If it features in Heaven, it must feature in any garden that seeks to re-create Heaven. And so it does. Water is an essential feature of many of the gardens in this book, because it symbolizes the life force. The Chinese, Persian, Renaissance, and Zen gardens must all have water. It is a common feature in other gardens, too. This need runs deeper than mere symbolism. We know that water really does add a more spiritual element to any garden that we visit or create. The light reflected in it, or the sound of water running, lifts our spirits.

Trees, too, feature in many sacred gardens as a necessity. They represent the Tree of Life and, in a garden, they add a spiritual element of permanence that many smaller plants do not have – a permanence that Paradise itself possesses. Through the winter, when other plants die, evergreen trees demonstrate the triumph of life over death, just as Heaven offers a triumph over death. Once again, this is something that touches our spirits when we see a healthy tree, in full leaf, in the depths of winter.

Differences of Style

Although many of these features are common to several cultures, each has its own individual style, which reflects its own view of Heaven, as we shall see in this book. The Chinese, for example, were seeking to re-create the Mystic Isles where the Immortals lived, so they created a style of garden in which a lake was dotted with islands. The Zen gardens of Japan are an attempt to reproduce the

LEFT: The meditative aspect of gardening is nowhere better seen than in the calm and balance of the Zen garden.

harmony and balance of nature. In Persia and India, meanwhile, the Moguls built geometric designs of detailed symbolism.

To the medieval Christians, a garden was the home of the soul and a place of enlightenment; it was walled to protect and provide an escape from the troubles of earthly life. Its enclosed nature represented the feminine principle and, therefore, the protection of the Virgin Mary. The English wise woman worked in conjunction with nature, so her garden would be far more informal in style, maintaining a constant balance between her needs and those of nature.

European herb gardens were highly designed, each element of the design a reminder of the important elements of life, such as love and faithfulness. Art was central to life in Renaissance Italy, and its gardens aimed to balance art and nature in a way that reflected cosmic order. So each culture had its own way of re-creating Paradise on Earth. Some of these sacred gardens were places of meditation, some were refuges from the rawness of life, and others were places where sacred plants could be grown, to heal or refresh. We will look at each of these gardens in this book. They differ widely, but each of them offers us a view of Heaven, and an inspiration that we can still draw on today, hundreds or even thousands of years after they were first created.

Your own garden, whatever size, is your opportunity to express yourself through your vision of Paradise. Like you, it will be unique, whatever you choose to do with it. You may want a pleasure garden where you can share the company of friends, or an enclosed, safe space where you can escape from the world. You may want an uncluttered space where you can meditate, or somewhere that feels close to the wildness of nature. Or perhaps a garden

THE HANGING GARDENS OF BABYLON

According to tradition, King Nebuchadnezzar rebuilt the city of Babylon in about 600 B.C., and created the Hanging Gardens at its center. The gardens were raised on terraces supported by great stone arches, below the arches were garden rooms, and on top of them the soil was planted with trees. Babylon was in the center of a broad plain, but Nebuchadnezzar's wife came from a mountainous area, so her husband built the gardens to remind her of the land she had left behind.

The gardens may, however, never have existed. The first account of the gardens was written in the fourth century B.C., 200 years after the gardens were said to be built. There are no contemporary accounts of the garden at all. Perhaps the most famous gardens of all were only a dream of Paradise, and not its realization, after all.

THE GARDEN OF EDEN

....

And the Lord God planted a garden in Eden, in the east; and there he put the man whom he had formed. And out of the ground the Lord God made to grow every tree that is pleasant to the sight and good for food, the tree of life also in the midst of the garden, and the tree of the knowledge of good and evil. A river flowed out of Eden to water the garden, and there it divided and became four rivers...The Lord God took the man and put him in the garden of Eden to till it and keep it.

GENESIS, 2

in which to grow healing plants, or somewhere full
of scents – most people find the smell of flowers
uplifting when they are feeling stressed and dragged
down by the pressures and stresses of the everyday
world. Whatever your own personal choice, you can
learn from all the gardens in this book, and take
elements from each that will help you make your
own garden that much closer to Heaven.

The Garden of Eden was the ultimate Heaven on
Earth, created by God for Adam and Eve to live in.
Right up until the sixteenth century it was generally
assumed that Eden still existed somewhere on
earth, but had been lost after Adam and Eve were
banished from it. There were some people who
believed that Eden may have been washed away in
the flood that destroyed everyone except Noah and
his family, but no one doubted that Eden had once
had a real earthly location.

It is hardly surprising, therefore, that many
people wanted to find the Garden, and explorers in
the fifteenth century were eager to locate it.
Christopher Columbus searched for it when he
sailed west to the Americas, and he believed he had
found it when he reached South America. His
discoveries convinced him that he had located Eden;
the Gulf of Paria (on the northeast coast of
Venezuela) closely matched the biblical description
of the Garden of Eden.

However, there were problems. The Americas
contained plants and animals that were not
mentioned in the Bible. Worse, they were inhabited
by people who worshiped other gods. By the 16th
century, people were beginning to realize that the
Garden of Eden was nowhere to be found, and they
concluded that it must have been broken up and
scattered to the four corners of the Earth.

So, in order to re-create Eden, it would be
necessary to travel the globe collecting all the plants
that had been created and assembling them into
collections that would be, in effect, a catalog of the
contents of the Garden of Eden. Since God had
created plants to provide medicine in their leaves,
flowers, bark, or berries, any collection that
contained all the plants in the world must contain a
cure for every illness in the world.

This is how the first botanic gardens began in
Europe. They were the gardens of recreation –
literally – where people could see the plants that
grew in the first garden, and renew themselves
spiritually. After a time, this idea spread beyond the
scientific botanic gardens alone and became the
principle behind every recreational garden. Some
gardens are created to grow fruits or vegetables, or
for some other practical purpose. But a garden that
exists for recreation is just that: a re-creation of the
Garden of Eden.

*BELOW: Exotic plants are
collected for the botanic garden.*

CHAPTER ONE

TAOIST GARDENS

*T*he Chinese
Taoists believed
that the Immortals — humans who
had achieved immortality through
enlightenment — lived in the Mystic Isles. These were
mysterious islands hidden in the sea mists off the northeast
coast of China; only rarely did they appear, and they could
never be reached by humans. So the Chinese began to
re-create the Mystic Isles for themselves and
created a new style of garden that
aimed to emulate the perfect
land of the Immortals.

In about 140 B.C. the emperor Wu set out to find the Mystic Isles of the Immortals. He wanted to ask the Immortals to tell him how he too could achieve eternal life. The islands, however, were hidden in the sea mists, and after searching for a long time, the emperor finally had to abandon his search.

He wasn't prepared to give up yet. Instead he decided to try to lure the Immortals to the mainland by building a re-creation of the Mystic Isles for them. The Immortals never came and told Wu how to become one of them, but the traditional Chinese lake-and-island garden had been invented.

Some of the Mystic Isles were built on the backs of giant tortoises. The emperor Wu created a huge lake, with rocks and stones along the shore to imitate the sea coast. He constructed islands within the lake, some of them built on huge rocks to represent the tortoises. Around the lake he created simulated mountains out of more rocks, on which he built palaces and pavilions to attract the Immortals, interconnected with bridges. His entire gardens are said to have covered 50 square miles (30 sq km). Wu imported animals to fill his gardens – camels, peacocks, monkeys, elephants, wolves, and many others. He created a miniature empire, a complete landscape to attract the Immortals.

For a while, Chinese gardens became ever more elaborate. By the sixth or seventh century A.D. they reached their peak. One emperor had a garden that included lakes with dragon-headed barges carrying orchestras of concubines. The lotus flowers on the lakes never faded, and in the winter, silk flowers were tied to the bare branches of the maple trees. However, by the twelfth century the mainstream style of Taoist gardens had returned to a more nature-loving design.

Reflecting Nature

Taoism is a nature religion; its followers believe that everything in nature contains its own spirit — each mountain, stream, and stone. Since their deities reside in natural objects, creating gardens that represent nature is the Taoist way of re-creating places fit for the gods to live, just as the emperor Wu tried to do.

Taoist gardens are a reflection of the natural landscape, often scaled down. They may contain many buildings and bridges, but these exist to help the visitor view the garden landscape from the best possible angle. The Buddhists, followers of one of China's other main belief systems, have many holy mountains. The paths up these mountains tend to be dotted with temples and resting places, but these are carefully positioned to allow the pilgrim to see a particularly beautiful work of nature — a wonderful view or a spectacular waterfall.

The Taoists borrowed this practice, although they often manufactured the "works of nature" themselves. They would go to great lengths to select the perfect rocks to build their artificial mountains and great expense to excavate their ponds and lakes. They constructed grottoes and planted trees, and created miniaturized landscapes.

Into these landscapes they put buildings, which helped the visitor to appreciate the view, or improved the feng shui — the natural geomancy — of the garden. Often, too, there were boats from which the scenery could be appreciated.

The Garden of Perfect Brightness

One garden, created for the summer palace of one of the emperors in the 18th century, was called the Garden of Perfect Brightness. This contained artificial hills 50 to 60 feet (15-18m) high, with numerous small valleys created between them. Water had been channeled through these valleys in a series of rivers, waterfalls, pools, and lakes, landscaped with rocks and stones so as to appear natural. Visitors were conducted in barges through these valleys in a winding route. The slopes of the valleys were dotted with grottoes and pavilions from which to view the scenery.

This may sound like the height of artifice, and so it is in a sense, but it was also a sincere attempt to emulate the best and most perfect aspects of the natural world that the Taoists revered.

LEFT: Rocks and water were essential symbolic elements in the gardens of ancient China and Japan. Interconnecting bridges had their own symbolic value.

RIGHT: The harmony of the contrasting elements of nature were emphasized by the careful positioning of a building such as a pavilion.

Over the centuries, gardens stopped being the prerogative of emperors and nobles and began to be built – on a humbler scale – by ordinary people. The principles were exactly the same although the gardens were scaled down. They still copied or emulated nature on a reduced scale with water, islands, buildings, and bridges. Their function was to create a private retreat for simple contemplation and meditation, and they contained features to encourage this.

Since the Taoists believe that every object in nature contains its own spirit, each feature is designed and placed with the maximum respect. Rocks, trees, plants, and fish are all treated with the utmost care, and to be alone in a Taoist garden is to be surrounded by earth spirits.

RIGHT: A Chinese garden could be created by adapting the natural landscape as well as by imitating it.

THE ART OF FENG SHUI

Feng shui is Chinese geomancy; the ancient art of reading the landscape and adjusting the surroundings and any building, decorating or planting, to maximize the positive energy flow and generate good fortune.

The Taoists believe that everything contains ch'i, or energy, and that the ch'i in the atmosphere must be allowed to flow freely. If allowed to stagnate, or to accelerate too fast, it creates an unhealthy effect such as poverty, bad luck, or illness.

Feng shui is a complex art, taking into account the direction from which the ch'i flows, the section of the garden or property in question, the way the garden faces, and a number of other factors. Feng shui consultants were employed, and still are, to advise people on how to generate the greatest good luck for themselves, but the basic principles of feng shui are relatively simple.

Ch'i likes to flow in smooth curves, so there should be no straight edges to any of the natural features of the garden such as ponds or paths. It will stagnate in dead ends or dark corners, but this can be remedied if the area is brightened up with light or water to create reflections – this helps the ch'i to find its way back out. If it is funneled down narrow paths or gaps between buildings or other features, it will become dangerously fast. The solution to this is to slow it down by curving the path or breaking up the straightness with wind chimes or plants. This is the reason that Chinese buildings often have upturned eaves: to prevent the ch'i from plunging off the roof, and encourage it instead to run gently off the edge.

The position of the garden in the landscape as a whole is important to the Taoists, and feng shui consultants would advise on the best location to build a house and garden. Ideally it should have high protective hills to the north, gentle hills to the east, and should slope away gently to the south, and have a river protecting it to the west.

Pagodas were commonly built on hills overlooking towns to help improve the feng shui of the locality and prevent disasters such as floods. They had many upturned eaves and were often decorated with wind chimes. The gardens in the town would be made so that the view in the direction of the pagoda was kept open, so allowing the ch'i to flow in and out of the garden.

PALACE GARDEN OF PEACEFUL LONGEVITY,
BEIJING

This is an elegant but simple garden in the Forbidden City. Its main features are its huge rockeries or artificial mountains. These rockeries were carefully designed, and many of them were copies of mountains in Chinese paintings. The garden also contains many ancient trees and several beautiful buildings. One of these buildings, approached by a path of natural rock steps, is the Pavilion of Ceremonial Purification. The emperor Qian Long, who ruled in the late eighteenth century, was a lover of poetry and used to hold evenings of poetry recitals with his closest companions here. The pavilion contains a stone floor into which a watercourse has been carved in the shape of the ru yi symbol, which means "anything you desire." A wine cup would be floated along this channel and whoever it stopped in front of would have to recite a poem.

RIGHT: *In the Taoist gardens of the Beijing Summer Palace the bridge forms a perfect place from which to admire the garden by day or night, as well as creating a link, and being an important visual element in its own right.*

GARDEN OF HARMONIOUS PLEASURES,
BEIJING

This is part of the Garden of Ease and Harmony at the New Summer Palace. The Garden of Harmonious Pleasures was built by Qian Long as a copy of a garden he saw on a visit to southeast China in 1751. Many imperial gardens contain features that have some spiritual or philosophical reference. This garden contains a small bridge called the Understanding Fish Bridge. This refers to a conversation between a Taoist master and a Confucian scholar who were standing on a bridge. The Taoist master said to his companion: "Look at the fish enjoying themselves." The Confucian scholar replied: "How do you know they are enjoying themselves?" His Taoist friend responded: "How do you know that I don't know that they are enjoying themselves?"

THE LODGE OF THE QUIET HEART,
BEIJING

At the start of the twentieth century, this was one of the favorite gardens of the Empress Dowager. It is an enclosed, secret garden centered on a pool surrounded by artificial hills. There are many closely spaced halls and pavilions, and winding paths. Around the back of the garden is a covered walkway from which the garden can be viewed. The buildings all have plain roofs made from unglazed tiles, but there is a grander element in the red painted columns.

THE COMPONENTS OF THE TAOIST GARDEN

Water

Water is almost always the central focus of the Taoist garden. Traditionally, if there was no natural spring in the garden, water would be brought in from the nearest supply by digging out channels for it. Although many gardens were flat, water was often piped to create artificial waterfalls.

There are two ways of using water in a Taoist garden. One is to create a central pool as a focus for the garden; the other is to have a series of streams and waterfalls running through ravines and valleys.

Pools and lakes are highly valued because of their reflective qualities, which aid meditation. For this reason the open space of water is not broken up by bridges or by plants such as water lilies but is left empty and complete, although water plants might be grown around the edges. Fish beneath the water, however, are a positive help to meditation, so gold and silver carp are often kept in garden pools.

Lakes and pools should, of course, be of a natural shape, so there should be no straight edges or hard lines. Earth banks are ideal, but in China where the rains can be very heavy they were often hard to maintain. The popular alternative was to use piles of rocks or boulders along the banks, interplanted with small trees or creeping plants. These rocks should be placed so as to create as natural a view as possible, with the craggier boulders at the top of the bank and the flatter stones at the shore of the pool.

Mountains

Rocks are another essential feature of the Taoist garden. These are used to create mountains. Sometimes a large single rock will be placed to represent a mountain. Often piles of rocks will be used. Since each rock contains its own spirit, it must be carefully placed. It was always accepted that from close up it would be possible to tell that these hills and mountains were artificial – often the mortar joining the rocks would be visible – but from a distance they should appear quite natural, even if the more modest ones were closer to mounds or hillocks than mountains.

These mountains could be left as bare rock, interplanted with trees or shrubs, or covered with earth with a few select boulders placed on top to create the rocky peaks. A winding path of steps was often built to allow the visitor to climb to the top. Where the mountains were large enough, they might even have a pavilion placed on top, although this should not dominate the mountain but simply provide a place from which to observe the view.

The artificial mountains in Taoist gardens often had grottoes hollowed out in the base, with a pool in the cool dark hollow, or a waterfall in front of it. Special rocks would be chosen to line the grotto, ones with many pitted holes and worn with age. The largest of these grottoes might be as big as eight feet (2.5 m) across, large enough for people to sit inside. Many, however, would be smaller and designed to be viewed from the outside.

Buildings and Bridges

Buildings are an important part of Taoist gardens. In a small or medium-size garden they would often take up about a third of the ground space; in a large garden they would account for perhaps half this much of the space.

There are several kinds of buildings found in Taoist gardens. These buildings were always functional; they were designed for viewing the best aspects of the garden from a particular angle. Some imperial gardens had incredibly elaborate structures, but the most spiritual of the Taoist

ABOVE: The focus of a Taoist garden is a pool of water containing fish as an aid to meditation.

gardens contained far more simple versions of the buildings. The style would be clean and simple, often rustic, although the buildings would frequently also include a section of elaborate carving such as a screen or a door.

These buildings would traditionally be made from dark timber with bamboo or timber screens or whitewashed walls, and slate tiles on the roof. The white walls serve as a visual foil to trees and plants, and also help to reflect light. Many buildings have removable latticework screens. These create glimpses of a long-distance view through the close-up detail of the carved lattice. When the screen is removed, the longer view across the garden – and perhaps beyond – is revealed fully. The red and gold structures often associated with Chinese gardens belong to the era of elaborate imperial parks and gardens, rather than to the more spiritual and simply designed Taoist gardens.

There are several types of buildings particularly favored in Taoist gardens:

Verandas: open-fronted structures, often attached to the side of a house, with a solid roof.

Dry boats: these are open-fronted, veranda-type

ABOVE: Set among trees and shrubs, a Chinese garden pavilion provides a resting place for the eye as well as for the body.

structures built to project out over the edge of a lake so you can look down into the water and contemplate the reflections.

Pavilions: enclosed buildings similar to summerhouses; the windows are often half covered with latticework shutters or screens.

Gazebos: these are open-sided buildings, sometimes with the roof also open, and they frequently have eight sides.

Covered walks: these can be open-sided, but they are often walled with openings in the shape of flowers or fans through which the garden can be glimpsed.

Bridges could be constructed of wood, but often they were designed to appear natural, created from long flat stones laid across streams. Sometimes a chain of these is laid in a zig-zag across the corner of a pool, although never across the middle where it would break up the expanse of clear water.

Bridges not only allow access across water, they are platforms from which to contemplate the reflection of the clouds in the water, or the fish slowly swimming beneath the surface. A garden with stone lanterns on the bridge can be appreciated at night, where the reflection of the lights imitates the reflection of the moon. Never cross a bridge without lingering for a while to look at the view before you reach the other side.

Flowers

Although China has a wealth of flowers occurring naturally, relatively few are used in their gardens. This is chiefly because their gardens are not so much the domain of botanists but of artists and poets. The plants that they do use are chosen for their shape or their scent rather than for their color, although white flowers are most popular. They tend to be planted in large groups and drifts, not interspersed singly.

Plum trees, and other trees with spring blossom, are often planted at the foot of artificial "mountains" to represent clouds, with the head of the mountain appearing above them.

Contrast

In order to create good feng shui, a balance of yin and yang must be incorporated into the garden. This is created by contrasts of short and long views together, or simple and ornate designs on buildings, such as a simple veranda of clean, straight lines but with ornate carvings where the posts meet the roof. Taoist gardens also contrast rough and smooth, mountain and plain, upright and horizontal, by placing them close together.

Contrast is also created by juxtaposing light and shade, so that a shady spot will be created in the brightest part of the garden, or a tree will be planted to cast a dark shadow onto a whitewashed wall. These features are not accidental in Taoist gardens but are an integral part of the design.

Borrowed Views

These contrasts within Chinese gardens include juxtaposing closeup and long-distance views. The Chinese create windows in walls to open up a distant panorama, or prune the branches of trees to allow the viewer to see far-off trees and mountains as well as those nearby. If you are creating a Taoist garden in a small space this is a useful feature to employ, allowing the wider view to contrast with the enclosed space within the garden.

The Simple Path

The great Taoist philosopher Lao Tzu, who is thought to have lived in the sixth century B.C., explained Wu Wei – the Simple Path – in a way that is reflected in all Taoist gardens. He described the path thus: "This is the Simple Path: to return to the simplicity and naturalness we once had. The path of the breeze that gently whispers through the trees, of the bird that climbs into the open, clear blue sky. The way of the simple flowers that blossom without effort and through Wu Wei catch the warmth and blessing of the sun. The way of the waters that run through the veins of the earth, overcoming obstacles without effort, and pass at last into the wide ocean…To feel Wu Wei is to know the inner pulse of the Tao, which is reality itself."

BELOW: All of nature is balanced and harmonized in the Taoist garden, enabling the mind to be at peace.

PEACH
immortality; the god of
long life is often
depicted holding a peach
from his tree, which
bears fruit once every
3,000 years

WATER LILY
purity and truth

THE SYMBOLISM OF FLOWERS

The most popular flowers include peonies,
day lilies, orchids, hollyhocks, tiger lilies,
yellow chrysanthemums, water lilies, and
the lotus. Shrubs include bamboos,
hydrangeas, roses and tree peonies, and
the favorite tree is the plum. Other trees
include the Japanese apricot, peach,
cherry, crab apple, magnolia, mulberry,
and pine. Many of these have symbolic
meanings

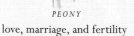

PEONY
love, marriage, and fertility

BAMBOO
the jointed sections of the straight stems represent
the steps along the path to enlightenment

MAGNOLIA
beauty and gentleness; this tree once belonged to the emperor alone, and to have one growing in your garden meant you had been honored by a gift from the emperor himself

CHERRY
spring and youth

PLUM
the flower is the emblem of winter, and the fruit represents female sexuality

CHRYSANTHEMUM
long life, prosperity, and contemplation

CREATE YOUR OWN
TAOIST GARDEN

*I*f you want to create a Taoist garden in a relatively small space you can do so. It isn't necessary to build a real mountain; you can use rocks to represent it.

All the elements of the great Taoist gardens can be scaled down to suit a smaller space. This garden incorporates all the essential elements of a classic Taoist garden, but on a small enough scale to include in an average-size garden.

KEY

1 Central pool containing koi

2 Paved area at entrance to house

3 Raised flower beds containing chrysanthemums at the front and peonies at the back. Flowers are usually grown near buildings in rectangular beds, often either raised or sunken

4 Lilies growing in pots

5 Stone flagged path to pavilion

6 Roofed pavilion with latticework screens in the sides with larger openings from which the pool and the artificial hills can be viewed

7 Plum trees

8 Stone bridge with stone lanterns on pillars at each end

9 Artificial mounds of earth with rough boulders projecting from the earth (you can create these from the earth dug out to make the pool)

10 Wisteria planted between boulders

11 Pine trees

12 Open-fronted pavilion or "dry boat" projecting over edge of water for viewing pool

13 Hydrangea bushes

14 Water lilies at edge of pool only, so as not to obscure the view of open water

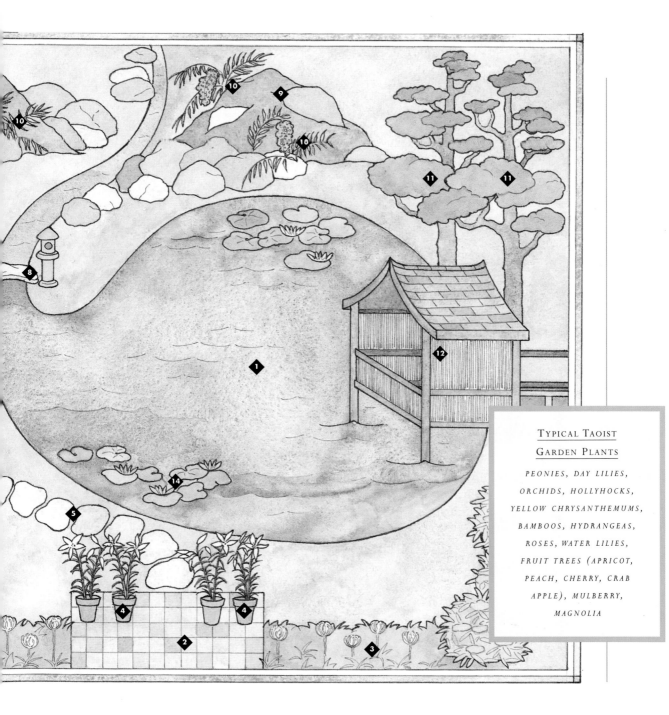

TYPICAL TAOIST
GARDEN PLANTS

*PEONIES, DAY LILIES,
ORCHIDS, HOLLYHOCKS,
YELLOW CHRYSANTHEMUMS,
BAMBOOS, HYDRANGEAS,
ROSES, WATER LILIES,
FRUIT TREES (APRICOT,
PEACH, CHERRY, CRAB
APPLE), MULBERRY,
MAGNOLIA*

CHAPTER TWO

ZEN GARDENS

There is an Eastern saying that a sacred space is only complete when you can take nothing more away from it. The Japanese Zen garden is a triumph of simplicity, in which the balance of nature is emphasized, to create a space of stillness and meditation. The first Zen gardens were created by Zen Buddhist monks as places of contemplation. They distilled the Chinese style of gardening, which had already been adopted into Japan, down to its simplest form.

he Japanese garden aims to emulate the beauty of the natural landscape to create something that is not only esthetically pleasing but also practical. In particular, the Japanese garden is a place of tranquility where you can meditate. The very first source of Japanese garden design was the sacred shrines they built to their gods, which were simply clearings in the forests, covered with sand and edged with rope, to encourage the divine spirits to come down to earth and bless the crops.

Much of the art of gardening was introduced to Japan from China in the seventh century A.D., and early Japanese gardens were similar to Chinese gardens. They often incorporated, however, more of the simplicity of those first shrines, so their predominant style was less elaborate than that of the Chinese.

In the twelfth century, the samurai warriors rose to power. They followed the path of Zen Buddhism, which believed in austerity, humility, and simplicity as the route to enlightenment. Zen priests were highly skilled in the arts, including gardening, and they introduced a style of their own. Zen gardens were, and still are, places for contemplation, where the power of nature is emphasized, humbling our own brief human existence. When tea was first imported from China, it was the Zen priests who devised the tea ceremony. The ritual was originally designed to help them stay awake while meditating, which they often did for hours at a time.

The early Zen gardens were often lush with water, moss, and trees. At the other extreme, Zen gardens can contain nothing but rocks and gravel — the classic "dry garden." But even the more heavily planted gardens had a Zen simplicity about them,

LEFT: Waterfalls in Zen gardens represent the Buddhist god Acala, and Zen priests will make offerings to the deity.

and incorporated some elements of the dry garden. There would be, for example, a stream or waterfall constructed from gravel and rocks as well as a real stream or lake somewhere else in the garden.

The Principle of Balance

The aim of the Zen garden is to create a perfect harmony of yin and yang. These are the two complementary principles of Chinese philosophy, which were adopted by the Zen Buddhists. Everything in the universe is influenced by these two forces; yin is the feminine, dark, negative, passive, cold aspect of nature, while yang is the masculine, light, positive, active, hot aspect. All things can be divided into either yin or yang, although everything contains an element of the other since neither can exist alone. This is why the Chinese yin-yang symbol contains a dot of white in the black yin, and a dot of black in the white yang.

In a Zen garden, there is water and land. Water is yin and land is yang. In a dry garden, the raked gravel or sand represents water, and the rocks represent islands or mountains. The art of the gardener is to create a garden in which these two elements are in perfect balance. It is because the gravel or sand in a dry garden represents water that it is raked into patterns. These shapes are not abstract, but indicate the ripples or waves of water lapping around the island rocks.

Those gardens that incorporate shrubs — which not all of them do — use azaleas, cut-leafed maples, conifers, and bamboos to represent land, or yang. Moss is used as a substitute for yin water.

Although all this makes the creation of a true Zen garden a challenging task, there is still one more factor to consider. The finished garden must celebrate nature, and even transcend it if possible. The Zen garden represents nature in its most harmonious form, so the final design must give the overall impression of being a natural, not a contrived, creation.

Creating Permanence

The Western idea of gardening almost always celebrates the changing seasons. It is a feature of many gardens that a particular part of it is, for example, carpeted with snowdrops in the early spring, and by the late summer is a blaze of flowers in hot shades of red and orange. The Japanese, on the other hand, have a completely different approach. They are striving to create the perfect balance of yin and yang. Once they achieve it, the last thing they want to do is to upset it with a new array of plants as the season changes.

The perfect Zen garden never changes at all, and many of the gardens in Japan are still exactly as they were when they were first designed centuries ago. The same stones stand in the same places, and the gravel is still raked exactly as it always has been. This is one of the reasons that conifers are popular in Zen gardens: they don't change with the passing seasons in the way that deciduous trees do.

The only thing allowed to change in a purist garden is the surface of the stones. As the centuries pass, they slowly collect mosses and lichens and acquire a patina of age, which adds to their character and makes them highly respected and valued.

BELOW: The natural harmony between yin and yang is reproduced in the ideal Zen garden.

ZEN STONES

Stones play a hugely important part in the Zen garden. Many of these gardens contain only stones (representing yang land) and gravel (for yin water). The art of using stones has become highly developed, and there are five principal shapes of stone that can be used in a classic dry garden: two vertical and three horizontal.

Vertical stones

Statue stone: this should be tall, with a cone-shaped top and a bulge in the middle.

Low vertical stone: this is taller than it is wide, but not as tall as the statue stone.

Horizontal stones

Flat stone: this is an irregular-shaped, flat stone, higher than a stepping stone.

Arching stone: this is a medium-height stone that arches over to one side at the top.

Recumbent ox stone: this is a long stone that is higher at one end than the other.

Stones can be used on their own, or in groups of two, three, or five. There are traditional situations where certain combinations tend to be used; for example, you often see a statue stone and a flat stone together at the edge of a stream (whether real or gravel). The statue, low vertical, and recumbent ox stones are often grouped together on the side of a hill.

Stones contain their own spirit and have their own personality, and it is important to work with this when you place the stone. Each stone is said to have six faces, and it is important to choose the right face to look toward the visitors to the garden.

The arrangement is never random, however much it may seem so. Sometimes there may even be groupings of stones in which one or more is completely submerged from view, but its presence is still important. Stepping stones slow people down as they approach the tea house, but although their arrangement is irregular, it is carefully planned. If the stones form the wrong shape, smaller stones, known as throwaway stones, are added to the design to redress the balance. These are never walked on.

The eleventh-century gardening treatise, *Sakuteiki*, says: "For each leaning stone there must be a supporting stone; for each running away stone, a pursuing stone; for each upward-looking stone, a downward-looking stone; for each upright stone, a horizontal stone."

An improperly sited stone can produce a lack of harmony in the gardener's own life, and is therefore unlucky. Stones with misshapen tops are diseased; vertical stones lying flat are dead; and randomly strewn stones are poor. In the wrong position a stone can even assume the shape of *ishigami* or "demon stone." However, if you listen to the spirit of the stone it will always tell you where and how it should be placed.

RYOAN-JI, KYOTO,
JAPAN

This is arguably the most famous dry Zen garden in the world. It is contained in a rectangular enclosed garden, which has a wooden veranda running along one side; this is the viewing platform. The garden is about 500 years old and consists of 15 rocks, arranged in groups, on a raked gravel bed. The gravel itself is still raked into the same patterns as it has been for centuries.

Originally the garden contained no greenery at all, but over the years the stones have acquired a covering of moss. The purpose of the garden is to stimulate the mind in meditation, but it is best visited in the early morning for this, since it is crowded with tourists and visiting schoolchildren later in the day.

HUNTINGDON BOTANIC GARDENS
SAN MARINO, CALIFORNIA, USA

This is a dry-type Zen garden within a Japanese garden. It is surrounded by an earth-colored wall with a tile capping and has a slate walk from which the garden can be viewed. This can be taken to represent the bank of the "stream" that is suggested by the gravel as it flows around the rocks in its path.

The gravel stream is backed by trees and shrubs that represent the far bank of the stream. One of the shrubs has been clipped into a square shape as a contrast intended to provoke thought and meditation. The whole garden distills the atmosphere that rocks and real water might produce.

THE COMPONENTS OF
THE ZEN GARDEN

The classic Zen garden is composed of up to five main elements: stone, sand or gravel, water, plants, and space. Not all five of these have to be present, but any Zen garden must contain either the yin of water or sand or gravel, and the yang of either stone or plants. All Zen gardens must also have a sense of space: where a garden is cramped or cluttered the natural energy of nature cannot flow freely around it.

Stone

Stones are the solid, yang element of the Zen garden and balance the yin of raked gravel or water. Their character and shape is extremely important, and complex rules have been developed as to their placing. The age of stones is a strong part of their personality, and it is therefore extremely important that only real stones are used. You cannot create a Zen garden that is in balance if you use synthetic or reconstituted stone.

As well as placing rocks in the garden to represent islands and mountains, you can also introduce stone in the form of stepping stones leading to the tea house, or a hollowed stone washbasin with a carved stone lantern over it to use when you visit the tea house at night.

Plants

Zen garden plants are never functional. They are not there to be harvested or eaten, but as an integral part of the design. Pine trees are very popular because they are easy to prune and train to create an effect of age and weather relatively early in their lives. The Japanese have a huge reverence for age and for the ancient things of nature, such as stones and long-lived trees.

The Japanese also like to use maple trees because they are deciduous, although this means

BELOW: Over the course of time mosses and lichens accumulate on the rocks of a Zen garden adding to the sense of permanence.

that the garden loses a little of its sense of permanence. What it gains instead is a reminder of the cycle of life and death, and maple leaves, while continually cleared from the ground in most places, will sometimes be left beside a stone basin, or at the edge of a path, to remind visitors of the transience of human life.

Bamboo can also be used in Zen gardens, but with care since it is an invasive plant. Other popular Japanese plants, such as azaleas, cherry trees, and plum trees, are seldom seen in Zen gardens. Nor do Zen designs include anything as transient as the iris and chrysanthemum flowers, so popular in other styles of Japanese garden. They do, however, incorporate grass and moss; moss grows particularly well in the humid climate of Japan.

Water

The earliest form of Japanese gardens were Shinto shrines (Shinto is the ancient religion of Japan). Water was essential for purification rituals, and it has been a vital ingredient in Japanese gardens ever since, although the later dry gardens used gravel and sand to represent it, rather than using the real thing. Japan is a country made up of islands, and this gives them a huge respect for water. It also explains why so many Japanese gardens include stretches of water with islands in them.

Since the Zen garden is designed to reflect nature, water is always used in natural shapes, never in geometric designs, even when it comes from an artificial supply. Stagnant water should be avoided at all costs; the movement of the water is an essential part of its function in the garden.

Ideally, water should come from the east side, flow under the house, and then across the garden toward the southwest. This cleanses any evil spirits from the west (traditionally the direction of the white tiger) with the waters of the blue dragon of the east and confers health and longevity to the owner of the house.

The Japanese Buddhist deity Acala said that any waterfall three feet (1 m) high represented his body. So Zen gardens often contain waterfalls of three feet (1 m) or more, and symbolize the Buddhist trinity by placing two vertical stones at the base of the cascade to represent Acala's attendants.

Zen gardens often look their best after the rain, and it is not uncommon to sprinkle water on stones, especially those leading to the tea house, in order to bring out their patina and texture. The

yang stones need the addition of a drop of yin water to create the complete effect.

Sand or Gravel

Even before dry gardens were developed, gravel played an important part in Japanese gardens. Early shrines were simply clearings covered with white gravel or sand, and later on, the courtyards of the imperial palaces were completely covered with vast expanses of gravel.

Gravel or sand is raked to represent wave patterns in water, and their fluidity when used in this way is an important part of their use. They are the yin, or feminine, element of the garden. Sometimes overlapping flat pebbles are laid to represent the course of a stream. Sand is used less often because it tends to blow away; it is suitable only in sheltered, contained areas. It is most commonly used in courtyard gardens, where it can give a greater sense of space than gravel.

Gravel should not be too coarse, or too dark in color, since both of these inhibit the sense of fluidity. Usually white or pale gray gravel is used. White gravel introduces more light (which is yang) into the garden, while dark gravel exerts a yin influence. So the color of the gravel will influence the balance of the garden.

You can create variety by using different sizes of gravel, or even different colors. However, muted colors create the most natural effects, and you must always remember that simplicity is crucial in a Zen garden. The harmony will be lost if you try to mix too many colors or sizes, or to create too complex a pattern.

LEFT: However large or small the garden, winding pathways lead the visitor from one part to another, urging us on to hidden areas.

THE TEA GARDEN

Before the introduction of Zen gardening, tea houses were a common feature of Japanese gardens, but in the fifteenth century the Zen monk Shuko Murata developed the *wabi* tea ceremony. Tea houses had been grand and impressive before, but the Zen approach was to create a hut that emphasized the rustic and the humble. The object of the tea ceremony is to remove yourself for a while from the everyday world and to focus on the essential things in life.

The ceremony begins with the approach to the tea hut through the tea gardens. It is important to focus on details to sharpen the mind, so the style of the path is important. It should consist of a series of detailed views, with twisting paths and stepping stones to slow your pace to the speed suitable for meditation and contemplation. Outside the door of the tea room is a stone washbasin, with a hollowed-stone lantern to light it at night, so you can wash your hands and your mouth before the ceremony begins. This ensures that you are purified in word and action. Sometimes a single maple leaf will be lying beside the basin to remind you of the cycle of life and death.

Humility is an important part of the ceremony. We cannot focus on what is important if our own egos get in the way. In order to symbolize the humility that is needed for the tea ceremony, the entrance to the tea room is so low that you must crawl to pass through it. Once inside, you are purified and humbled, and ready to contemplate and appreciate the simplest things in life.

Space

Space is not emptiness in a Zen garden; it is part of the overall design. It is essential to allow the spirit of nature to flow, and Zen gardens often open up spaces beyond their own boundaries. There will be a break in the fence or wall, or a branch carefully pruned from a tree, in order to open up a natural view beyond the garden itself.

Space in the garden is essential as an aid to meditation; many Zen gardens are designed to be viewed from specific vantage points, often where the sense of space is most accentuated. This allows you to clear your mind and free up the other senses. For example, it makes it easier to appreciate the sound of the breeze in the bamboo, or water flowing in the stream. The emptier the garden, the emptier your mind can be in preparation for reflection and meditation.

Meditating While You Work

Raked sand and gravel play an important role in meditation, not only when you sit contemplating the patterns but also as you create them. They require a huge amount of maintenance, so the Zen monks made the process of tending them a ritual in itself. Once you have established the pattern into which you rake the sand or gravel, it should be followed precisely, forever. If you concentrate completely on this, you can achieve flashes of enlightenment as you work.

A raked pattern will be destroyed every time there is a strong wind or heavy rainfall. To a follower of the Zen way, this doesn't matter. It is of no consequence that the garden looked perfect half an hour ago, or that it will look perfect tomorrow. The only thing that matters is what exists now. You simply pick the rake up and start again.

There are many different patterns you can rake gravel or sand into, to represent different types of wave patterns. In Japanese, each of these designs has its own name. There are large waves, scalloped waves, zigzag waves, ripples, and whirlpools. There is even a pattern known as "blue waves," which looks similar to fish scales, and indicates fish just below the surface of the gravel-water.

Whichever way you choose to rake the gravel, it should follow the natural flow that real water would. Rocks can have swirls and eddies around them, lakes can have calm, straight lines, and rushing streams can have waves and whirlpools.

LEFT: Contemplation is the aim of a true Zen garden, and uncluttered spaces created using simple, natural materials are conducive to this.

RIGHT: The Japanese garden pavilion was often a tea house, sacred to the tea ceremony. This building was set in a secluded part of the garden, approached by a winding path.

CREATE YOUR OWN ZEN GARDEN

*T*his is a design for a dry Zen garden that incorporates some greenery. The gravel represents water, but if you want real water you could add a stream flowing across the garden, winding through the gravel, into a pond. The stones and trees are positioned to be viewed from specific angles, especially the tea house and the garden entrance. The garden should be fenced or walled, with arches or gaps in the boundary if there is a natural view beyond it.

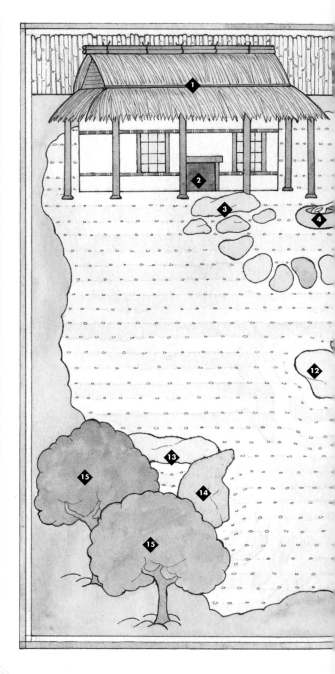

TYPICAL ZEN GARDEN PLANTS

CONIFERS, MAPLES, BAMBOO, MOSSES, LICHENS, SAXIFRAGE, CREEPING THYME

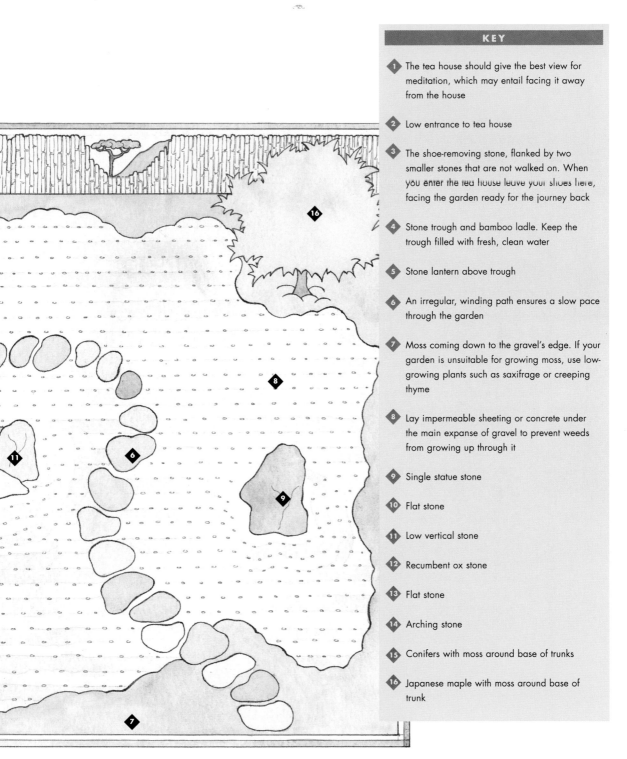

1. The tea house should give the best view for meditation, which may entail facing it away from the house

2. Low entrance to tea house

3. The shoe-removing stone, flanked by two smaller stones that are not walked on. When you enter the tea house leave your shoes here, facing the garden ready for the journey back

4. Stone trough and bamboo ladle. Keep the trough filled with fresh, clean water

5. Stone lantern above trough

6. An irregular, winding path ensures a slow pace through the garden

7. Moss coming down to the gravel's edge. If your garden is unsuitable for growing moss, use low-growing plants such as saxifrage or creeping thyme

8. Lay impermeable sheeting or concrete under the main expanse of gravel to prevent weeds from growing up through it

9. Single statue stone

10. Flat stone

11. Low vertical stone

12. Recumbent ox stone

13. Flat stone

14. Arching stone

15. Conifers with moss around base of trunks

16. Japanese maple with moss around base of trunk

UNIVERSITY OF WARWICK.
COVENTRY, UK

The Zen garden here is a dry garden, designed to represent the parable of the ox and the herdsman, which is an allegory for the stages of spiritual progress on the path to enlightenment. It was painted in the twelfth century in a series of ten pictures.

The story is told here in rocks and gravel. Large rocks represent the ox and the herdsman at various stages in the parable; the scenes are set within a circle of azalea bushes representing the circle of enlightenment. A dry stone river flows into a pond created from individually laid cobbles representing the movement of the water, and the whole garden has a backdrop of raked gravel.

ST. MUNGO MUSEUM
GLASGOW, SCOTLAND

St. Mungo's is a museum of religion, containing exhibits from different faiths. Among these is a Zen garden, created by Yasutaro Tanaka, a leading Japanese Zen garden designer from Kyoto. The garden consists of gravel, moss, and rocks and contains 15 rocks arranged in groups of seven, five, and three representing the prayer recited to Buddha repeated seven, five, and three times in succession. It can be interpreted in a number of different ways, one of the essential qualities of a true Zen garden.

DAISEN-IN, KYOTO,
JAPAN

....

This astounding garden is in the Daitoku-ji monastery. It is a three-dimensional copy of a Sung monochrome painting, created from stones, gravel, and sand. The painting itself is of a waterfall cascading into the ocean, with a bridge and a boat in the foreground. The garden, which is deceptively small (it is only 12 feet [3.6 m] deep), re-creates this without the use of water at all, but uses gravel of different sizes – along with sand and rocks – to represent the cascade of the waterfall and the pool at its base.

The garden deliberately deceives the eye into thinking that the water is moving, and that the boat is smaller than it is in relation to the rest of the landscape. This stands as a permanent symbol of the force of nature; the size of the boat serves to remind us that nature is more powerful than we are.

CHAPTER THREE

ISLAMIC GARDENS

*T*he Persians were great
garden builders, drawing
their inspiration from the need to create an
oasis of Paradise in their desert landscape. Their
gardens were a haven of order in a chaotic world. The
influence of the Persian gardens spread, along with Islam,
into India with the Moguls, and as far west as
Spain. From the Taj Mahal to the Alhambra,
the symbolism of Islam has left its
imprint on garden design.

*W*ater is essential in the dry deserts of Persia, and it is, therefore, the most essential feature of Persian gardens. Not only is it important for practical reasons, it also symbolizes life and is the purifying element. So water is always the central feature of the Islamic garden. The design of these gardens is very precise, and all classic Islamic gardens therefore look very similar in style. The aim was to re-create the garden of Paradise described in the Koran (trans. A. J. Arberry):

> This is the similitude of
> Paradise which the godfearing
> have been promised:
> therein are rivers of water unstaling,
> rivers of milk unchanging in flavor,
> and rivers of wine — a delight to the drinkers,
> rivers, too, of honey purified;
> and therein for them is every fruit,
> and forgiveness from
> their Lord…

LEFT: This Iranian garden at the tomb of Shah ne 'Matollan Vali is typical of the Islamic garden.

Islamic gardens therefore employ these four rivers, as channels or canals, flowing from a central pool or "tank" of water. This is often given a greater impression of depth by being lined with blue tiles. These channels divide the garden into four. The number four is the most holy number, and traditionally the number that symbolizes order and symmetry; it was important for the Persians to feel that they could impose order on an otherwise hostile terrain.

The gardens were often square but could be rectangular. Where they were much longer than they were wide there would often be a main channel or canal running the length of the garden, with a smaller channel crossing it at right angles. There might be more than one of these smaller channels in larger gardens, because it was necessary to repeat the pattern since it was important always to be within sight and sound of water.

The word "paradise" itself comes from the Persian meaning a walled garden, and Islamic gardens are always enclosed, usually within a high boundary wall. This geometric design was softened with trees and flowers. Fruit trees were planted, as described in the Koran, and cypresses, which symbolized both death and eternal life. Pines, palm trees, and almond trees were also popular. Flowers were grown in pots or geometrically shaped borders, often alongside the water channels. Since the flowering season in the desert is so short, color was also introduced into the garden with brightly colored tiles along the paths.

ABOVE: The Moorish invaders of Spain brought the "quartered" Islamic garden to Europe. Even where there is no real water flowing, the theme of the four rivers (of water, wine, milk, and honey), flowing from a central wellspring, is represented.

THE NUMBER FOUR

The number four had a huge significance to the Persians, dating from before Islam, and it was this number that was central to the design of their gardens. It draws on the traditional beliefs of many Middle Eastern religions.

According to the Hebrew tradition, in the Book of Genesis, "a river went out of Eden to water the garden and from there it parted and became four riverheads." Mesopotamian parks for hunting were divided into four with a central building because of their belief that the world was divided by four rivers. The Persians believed that the universe was divided into four squares with the wellspring of life at the center; the Koran states that Paradise is a garden flowing with milk, honey, wine, and water.

The cube represented not only order but also nature, or matter, while the circle symbolized Heaven. The interaction of these two essential patterns heavily influenced Persian architecture and hence their gardens, which were seen as an outdoor version of the same principle. This led to the classic "fourfold" or quadripartite Islamic garden, which was not only a place of relaxation but also an expression of understanding of the universe.

The Rose of Paradise

The most important of all flowers to the Persians was the rose; the yellow and red *Rosa foetida* was just one of the native varieties that bloomed for longer than any of their other flowers. Other varieties were introduced from China, to provide color in the garden when the other flowers had passed their season. The Persians had single and double shrub roses, musk roses *(R. moschata)*, and briar roses, in shades of white, pink, red, and purple. They even had yellow roses, a color provided by *Rosa hemisphaerica*

The rose took on a symbolic importance for the Persians. The Persian word for rose also means flower, so a flower garden was also a rose garden. Poets and philosophers used the rose as a motif and a metaphor. The thirteenth-century poet Sa'di wrote the *Gulistan*, translated as the *Rose Garden*. He considered his fragments of thought to be like rose petals collected from the garden of his meditations.

Roses were also planted to attract nightingales, which were seen as a symbol of love and longing – perhaps for the true Paradise – because of their plaintive song. Nightingales were associated with the moon because of their nocturnal habits; the crescent moon, along with the star, is still the symbol of Islam, and moongazing was an important activity in the Persian garden. The great Persian poet Omar Khayyám wrote in his *Rubaiyat* (trans. Edward Fitzgerald):

Ah, moon of my delight that knows no wane
The moon of heaven is rising once again.
How oft hereafter, rising, shall she look
Through this same garden after me in vain?

The Paradise Garden of the Assassins

It was claimed that the Old Man of the Mountains, the leader of the Persian sect of the Assassins in the eleventh and twelfth centuries, had a huge garden that was so closely modeled on the version in the Koran that it was thought to be Paradise itself. The Old Man trained his assassins to kill the great Christian leaders and the Saracens, by promising them the delights of Paradise as a reward, so the story went.

The Koran states that Paradise contains "maidens good and comely – houris, cloistered in cool pavilions – untouched before them by any man or jinn – reclining upon green cushions and lovely druggets…," and the Old Man had made sure that his Paradise lived up to this description. He reputedly gave his trainee assassins opium and, once asleep, had them carried to this garden where they would wake. Once persuaded by its delights that they never wanted to leave, they would be drugged again and removed to the palace. After this experience, they would do anything to regain their glimpse of Paradise.

Although there is probably only a little truth in this tale, it was believed to be true, which indicates the emphasis that the Arabs put on the promise of Paradise. The main account of this garden comes from Marco Polo who never saw it himself, but who wrote about it on the basis of the descriptions that he had heard on his travels.

RIGHT: Gardens are frequently depicted in Persian miniatures, indicating their significance in Persian civilization, and showing how carefully the plants were tended.

LEFT: A favorite flower in many cultures, the rose was especially important to the Persians.

ABOVE: Fruit trees and orderly beds characterize the Moorish gardens of Spain, such as the Medina area of the Alahambra gardens.

The Moorish Gardens of Spain

In the eighth century the Arabs conquered parts of Spain and brought with them their distinctive style of gardening. By the tenth century there were reckoned to be 50,000 villas around Cordoba, each with its own Paradise garden.

The Spanish gardens retained the essential design of the Persian gardens, but added their own style to it. For example, the central pool often became a lake with an elaborate pavilion at its center.

One of the preoccupations of the Arab garden builders was to integrate the gardens and buildings into one. The best surviving example of this is at the Patio de los Naranjos, or Court of the Orange Trees, in Cordoba, the oldest garden in Europe that still retains its original form. It is contained within a courtyard 130 yards by 65 yards (120 x 60 m), with a mosque at its center. The rows of orange trees along the water channels in the courtyard are exactly aligned with the rows of pillars within the mosque, creating as seamless a transition as possible from indoors to the open air.

The entrances to Persian gardens often incorporated highly decorated gateways, but the Moorish gardens of Spain have narrow and often twisting entranceways, symbolizing the road to Paradise. At the Alhambra Palace in Granada, the entrance to the Court of the Myrtles is through narrow passages within the thickness of the walls. This emphasizes the sudden brightness of the sunlight as one emerges into the Paradise garden.

THE PERSIAN CARPET

Persian rugs and carpets are important not only as floor coverings but also to cover doors and hang on walls, or even create partitions. One of the most common designs for Persian rugs was the garden, packed with symbolism drawn from the fourfold garden design. The flowering season in desert countries is so short that this was one way to bring the summer's colors indoors in the dry months.

These rugs are likewise divided into squares with straight patterns representing the rivers. The center of the rug often contains a representation of the central water tank, or perhaps a garden pavilion. Often there is a woven water channel running around the border of the whole rug. The border of Persian carpets used to be known by the Arab word for water; their word for earth was also used to describe the background of the carpet or rug.

Trees are often woven into the border design of the rug, encompassing the whole design with the representation of eternity. Flowers were woven in different colors – red, blue, green, and yellow – each representing a different element, season, division of the day, and division of human life.

One famous garden from the palace of Chosroes, who ruled in the sixth century A.D., was 100 feet (30 m) square. It was described at the time:

"The borders of the streams were woven in stripes, and between these borders tiny stones, the size of pearls, gave the impression of water. The stems and branches of the trees and flowers were woven from gold and silver; the leaves from silk like the rest of the plants, and the fruits from brightly colored stones."

RIGHT: One of the chief traditional designs for Persian carpets mirrors the design of an Islamic garden.

The Mogul Gardens of India

Islamic gardening reached its peak in India under the Mogul emperors. These Islamic invaders settled in northern India and constructed magnificent gardens on the same quadripartite design as those of Persia, Spain, and elsewhere. For nearly 200 years, throughout almost all of the sixteenth and seventeenth centuries, the Muslim emperor Babur and his descendants ruled northern India and the area around Kashmir and built some of the most beautiful gardens ever made. Babur made his capital at Agra, where the flat landscape called for a new style of gardens on a grand scale.

The main pool and fourfold channel design often had to be repeated in the garden with huge lakes, canals, and cascades. Flowers were usually grown around the water channels only in these gardens (largely for reasons of irrigation), and the rest of the garden would have long avenues of shady trees, and pergolas of vines, jasmine, and roses.

Some of the Mogul gardens were highly inventive, despite the fact that the basic design of the gardens seems restrictive. They vary hugely in both style and atmosphere, and the fourfold design seems to heighten rather than reduce their individuality. To give one example, the Moguls shared their Persian ancestors' love for spending time in the garden at night. One garden at the Red Fort in Delhi, which sadly no longer survives, was called the Mahtab Bagh, or Moonlight Garden. It was designed to be enjoyed at night, with niches behind each of the cascades, in which candles were placed. It was planted with pale, scented flowers —

LEFT: The Islamic invaders of northern India created magnificent gardens that were elaborate, ornamental, and grand, yet designed with geometrical simplicity. This is the lake garden at the Amber Palace in Rajasthan.

jasmine, lilies, and narsissus – which seem to glow in the light of the moon.

These grand gardens were often planted around a mausoleum, to represent the Paradise to which the departed spirit would go; the most famous of these Mogul gardens is the one around the Taj Mahal in Agra.

The word *bagh* means garden, and many of the great gardens were given the title *charbagh*, which literally means "four gardens" – a name that reflects the division of the garden into four by the water channels. The Mogul garden designers placed a building or structure at the outside end of each of the channels crossing the main channel in their larger gardens. This might be a gatehouse, a platform, or a pavilion, underneath which the water would flow away underground.

Providing water for these gardens was a huge challenge in the arid climate of India, and Mogul architects came up with ingenious ways to ensure a steady supply. In the gardens of the Taj Mahal the water was fed through underground pipes by a series of *purs* – a system of drawing water from the river using ropes and buckets pulled by bullocks. These *purs* brought the water from the river to a huge storage tank. It was then transferred via an overhead water channel to an even larger tank, by a series of 13 *purs*. Another 14 *purs* raise the water up to another set of tanks, one of which had the pipe mouths in its walls. These are the pipes that feed the gardens of the Taj Mahal.

Other complex engineering devices were then used to ensure that the water pressure in the fountains was uniform and consistent, so that all the water jets were continually aligned with each other. Not only garden design but also garden architecture and engineering were taken to an elevated form under the Moguls.

THE COMPONENTS OF THE
ISLAMIC GARDEN

Persian and Mogul gardens usually had magnificent gateways, often ornately carved or decorated. Many of the larger gardens had large gatehouses, such as the red sandstone gatehouse at the Taj Mahal. The Persian gardens, being totally enclosed, had solid gates or doors within their entranceways, and sometimes had four entrances, one in the center of each boundary wall.

Boundary

The Islamic garden was always enclosed, keeping out the dusts of the desert and capturing the scents and the coolness of the shade and the water. Ideally the boundary would be of stone, but it could be a thick hedge of cypress or some other evergreen tree; certainly it should be impenetrable.

BELOW: A plan of an Islamic-style garden, with typical rectangular, linear design, complete enclosure, and water in formal pools and channels.

Water

The central pool of water is essential, with four channels leading from it dividing the garden into the classic quadripartite design. The garden builders of Persia, and especially of India, constructed elaborate systems for feeding the tank with water and circulating it around the channels. It was usually fed from an underground spring, since much more of the water in Persia comes from the ground than comes from the sky.

The Moguls often grew sacred lotus plants in the central pool, but more often the water was left clear to reflect the surrounding buildings or the sky – symbolizing the garden as a reflection of Paradise.

The sound of water was as important as the sight of it, and water jets and little cascades in the channels helped to give this effect. In grander gardens, screens were specially constructed for the water to fall over.

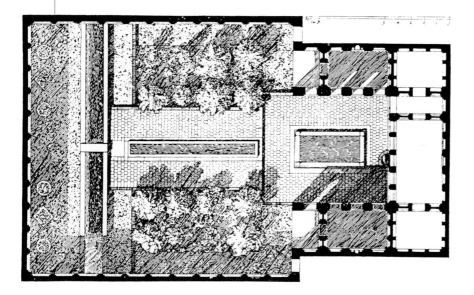

RIGHT: In this nineteenth-century garden of Paradise in Iran, green plants contribute to the cool shade of the palatial buildings, and both can be reflected in the calm expanse of water.

THE GARDEN OF HEART'S DELIGHT
SHIRAZ, IRAN

Shiraz has long been famous for its gardens; it is an oasis town in the desert that is full of trees and beautiful gardens. This garden has a pool and central channel bordered with long flower beds of roses and lilies, and numerous shady cypress and orange trees, and is a classic example of a Persian garden.

TOMB OF HUMAYUN
DELHI, INDIA

Many of the Mogul gardens extended the water channels into broad canals, but here they remain closer to the earlier style, only two feet (60cm) wide. A series of tiny channels distribute the water around the rest of the garden, connected by tiny cascades and rivulets. The water reaches the gardens down larger cascades fed by wells outside its boundaries. It is one of the most enchanting examples of an early Mogul garden.

TAJ MAHAL
AGRA, INDIA

This famous landmark, built by Shah Jahan in the seventeenth century as a tomb for his wife, is one of the greatest examples of a Mogul garden. It follows the fourfold design, divided by marble-lined canals. The white marble mausoleum is not in the center but at the north end of the main canal and is flanked by two red sandstone buildings. The garden also includes six sandstone pavilions and a gatehouse at the opposite end to the Taj Mahal itself.

When the Taj Mahal was first built the canals were bordered with avenues of cypress and fruit trees – symbolizing death and life – and the sunken beds were filled with flowers. The relationship between the mausoleum and the garden is a classic example of Islamic sacred geometry in practice; the overall effect is said by many people to be the most beautiful thing ever constructed by human hands.

NISHAT BAGH
LAKE DAL, KASHMIR

"The Garden of Gladness," this is perhaps the most spectacular of all Mogul gardens. It is arranged on 12 terraces, one for each sign of the Zodiac. The central canal runs down cascades at every change of level, and the canals and pools are full of fountains and water jets. This elaborate garden contains thrones and pavilions, avenues of trees, and colorful beds of flowers.

Gazebo

The word gazebo comes from the Persian and means a platform for viewing the moon. Originally gazebos were built in the corners of the garden and the Persians would sit, partly under cover, and view the moon and the stars. The gazebo would frequently have a central hole in the roof, usually square or rectangular, through which the sky could easily be seen.

Later, it became popular to build a platform above the central pool, reached by a bridge, which was used as a cool place to rest during the day as well as for viewing the night sky. As the development of gardens progressed, these became more ornate and were influenced by the design of Chinese pavilions. However, the Islamic version retained the viewing hole in the center of the roof.

BELOW: The Islamic devotion to gardens is reflected in the decorative arts; these tiles are from the Topkapi Palace in Istanbul.

Trees and Flowers

Shade was essential in a hot climate, and shady trees were always included. The most common of these were the oriental plane tree, the cypress, and, of course, the fruit trees mentioned in the Koran's description of Paradise.

Flowers were grown in sunken beds, often around the base of fruit trees. They would not have been planted in drifts but singly, and allowed to self-seed along with their companions. They would have included opium poppies, narcissus, anemones, mallow, fumitory, thyme, violets, and Madonna lilies. As well as roses, jasmine was grown to climb through trees and over buildings, adding scent to the garden.

Grape vines were often grown in Islamic gardens. One of the four rivers of Paradise described in the Koran was of wine, so this was regarded as the drink of the blessed. It was a common ingredient in these gardens designed to imitate Paradise itself.

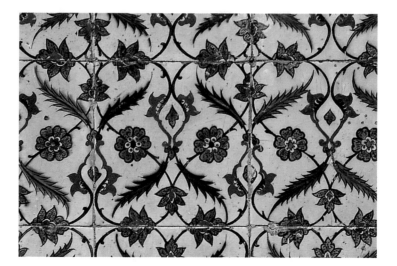

A Poet's Paradise

The garden represented the fruits of the soul as
well as the heavenly reward for earthly virtue.
The Persian poet Omar Khayyám used the garden
and its flowers as a metaphor for life and
its transience:

Look to the Rose that
blows about us - Lo
Laughing, she says,
into the world I blow;
At once the silken tassel of my purse
Tear, and its treasure on the garden throw.

As when the tulip for her morning sup
Of heavenly vintage from the soil looks up,
Do you devoutly do the like, till Heaven
To Earth invert you — like an empty cup.

Yet ah, that spring should vanish with the rose!
That youth's sweet-scented manuscript should close!
The nightingale that in the branches sang,
Ah whence, and whither flown again,
who knows?

*LEFT: In a Persian garden,
guests could enjoy flowers,
fruit, and music in the green
shade of the pavilion.*

CREATING AN ISLAMIC GARDEN

*T*his is a design for a classic quadripartite Islamic garden. It contains both cypresses, symbolizing death, and orange trees, symbolizing life. In colder climates the orange trees may not fruit, and it may be wise to protect them or bring them indoors over the winter months.

You can create this garden in a relatively small space, and you could scale it down if necessary by replacing the trees with shrubs, without losing the essential spiritual aspects of the design. Try using roses, myrtle, or box clipped into a simple ball shape, or small bush fruit trees.

TYPICAL ISLAMIC GARDEN PLANTS

ROSES, OPIUM POPPIES, NARCISSUS, ANEMONES, MALLOW, FUMITORY, THYME, VIOLETS, MADONNA LILIES, JASMINE, GRAPE VINES, FRUIT TREES (MORELLO CHERRY, ALMOND, APPLE, PLUM, ORANGE), PLANE TREES, CYPRESS

KEY

1. Central pool lined with blue tiles. For a more economical version, paint the lining of the pool and channels peacock blue

2. Water channels, fed from the central pool by small cascades, also lined with blue tiles

3. Flagstone paths (or you could use colored glazed tiles)

4. Sunken flower beds planted with shrub roses and anemones, narcissus, violets, mallow, southernwood, Madonna lilies, and opium poppies

5. Gazebo with open roof for viewing the night sky

6. Turf lawn

7. Orange trees planted in terra-cotta pots and clipped into balls

8. Cypress trees

9. Almond tree

10. Apple tree

11. Plum tree

12. Morello cherry tree. These fruit trees not only give shade to the garden but also symbolize the fruits of the soul

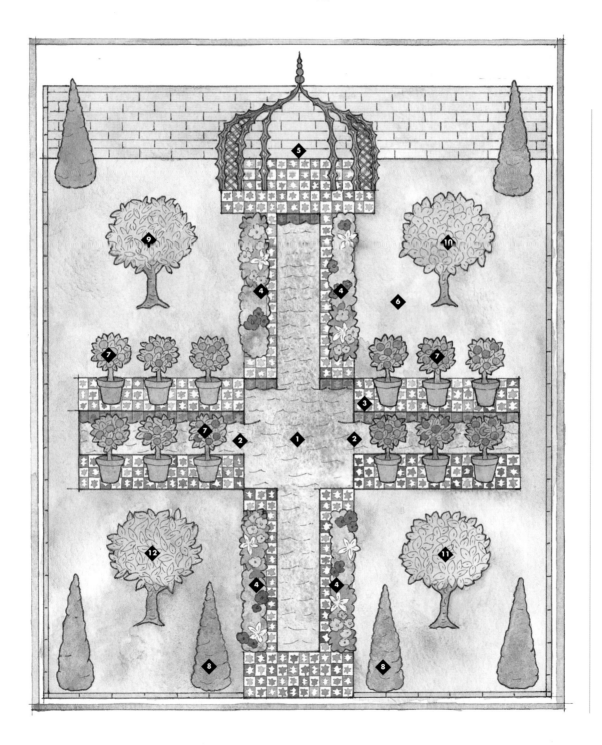

GENERALIFE
GRANADA, SPAIN

" The House of the Architect" stands on the
hillside above the Alhambra and is
about a hundred years older. Here the
courtyards are lushly planted in a
restoration of the likely original planting.
The Generalife contains the Patio de la
Riadh, the only garden left in Spain where
the wide stone-edged water channel runs
the entire length of the garden.

ALHAMBRA
GRANADA, SPAIN

O ne of the most famous sites in Spain, the Alhambra Palace was built by the Moors in the fourteenth century. It has four remaining garden courtyards, each very different, and yet each following the quadripartite design of the Islamic garden with a central water pool and channels leading from it. The Court of the Myrtles contains a central pool designed to reflect the surrounding buildings, which is flanked by clipped hedges of myrtle. The Court of the Lions has lost its original planting to be replaced by gravel, but it still has an orange tree in each corner, a beautiful fountain in the center, and four water channels.

Each of these courtyards is brightly sunlit and approached by a dark passageway from the interior of Heaven when one first emerges into Paradise.

CHAPTER FOUR

MEDIEVAL GARDENS

*M*edieval Europe
was a dangerous
place, full of lawless people and
terrifying diseases such as the Black Death. A
place of safety was essential for a peaceful life, and
the medieval garden with its protective surrounding walls
came to represent everything that was good and enlightened
in an evil world — a place of protection and retreat.
Medieval gardens followed a form of straight
lines and squares, to emphasize human
control over nature.

The art of gardening underwent a revival in the Middle Ages. The Romans had been enthusiastic garden builders across Europe, but when the Roman Empire fell, the art of gardening also collapsed. For several hundred years people farmed and grew a few culinary and medicinal plants, but there was no esthetic or spiritual element in the design of their gardens. It wasn't until the time of Charlemagne, in the early ninth century, that the gardener's skill was revived. The Emperor ordered every town in his kingdom to plant a garden of herbs with fruit and nut trees.

BELOW: *Walled gardens in mediaeval times might include a 'flowery mead' in which the women of the castle, palace or grand house enjoyed the beauty of the flowers and indulged in the pastime of garland weaving.*

The Song of Solomon

The inspiration the Christians took to adopt and develop these gardens came from the biblical Song of Solomon:

A garden enclosed is my sister, my spouse; a spring shut up, a fountain sealed. Thy plants are an orchard of pomegranates with pleasant fruits: spikenard and saffron, calamus, and cinnamon, with all trees of frankincense; myrrh and aloes, with all the chief spices.

The enclosed garden symbolized the womb and the feminine principle. It represented spiritual enlightenment, an escape from the trials of earthly life into a protected Heaven on Earth. It was sometimes situated within a larger walled garden, and was known as a *hortus conclusus*, which simply means "enclosed garden."

This feminine metaphor became associated with the beauty and purity of the Virgin Mary, and an even more studied style of garden was developed, known as the "Mary Garden." These gardens, while similar to other walled gardens, were planted specifically with flowers that had a symbolic meaning.

The most important flower of all was the rose. White roses were the emblem of the Virgin Mary because they signified her purity, while red roses represented the blood of Christ and of the martyrs. The single, five-petaled wild rose was also grown, as a symbol of Christ on Earth because the five petals form the shape of the human body with its arms and legs spread out. This fits into the shape of a five-pointed star representing divine love. So the

LEFT: *The medieval garden shares features in common with the Islamic garden, with its rectangular enclosure and its angular design. Herbs and edible plants were cultivated in its small, neatly arranged plots*

rose represents divine love in human form. The flower and the thorns of roses together represent mingled beauty and suffering. Roses were also grown for their hips, which were dried and strung together to make rosary beads.

After the rose, the next essential flower was the Madonna lily, also a symbol of the Virgin and, later, a symbol of the Annunciation. It was recorded that when the Virgin Mary ascended to Heaven her tomb was found empty except for lilies and roses. Violets were often grown in the grass to symbolize humility, along with daisies for innocence. Irises, with their three pairs of petals, symbolized faith, wisdom, and courage. Herbs were grown, such as rosemary, for faithfulness, and sage as yet another symbol of the Virgin. Other popular flowers included wild strawberries, hollyhocks, cowslips, and peonies.

ABOVE: Within its cloisters the medieval monastery had a formal, austere garden for contemplation, often arranged in four parts.

THE COMPONENTS OF THE MEDIEVAL CHRISTIAN GARDEN

Boundaries

Those who could afford it would have stone walls around their gardens or perhaps cob walls of straw and clay mixed together. Castle gardens were enclosed within stone walls and monastery gardens within stone cloisters. This gave strength to the garden's feeling as a place of retreat, protected from the evils of the world. Those affluent enough to have a garden, but not fortunate enough to be able to bound it with stone used fences or hedges, often surrounded by a ditch to keep livestock out. Hawthorn and holly were popular hedges, and willow, hazel, birch, alder, and oak were cut or coppiced to make fencing. Wattle fences were popular, and palisades of split oak or chestnut, or poles tied together in a square or diamond-patterned trellis design. As with the layout of the garden as a whole, geometric designs symbolized the taming of nature, which supported the Christian view that everything in nature was there for human benefit; an opposite view from that of the Taoist and Zen garden makers who sought to emulate and worship nature.

Paths

These were always simply made from turf, sand, or gravel. The choice of sand or gravel would depend on what was available locally rather than on any esthetic consideration. Low-growing, turf-like plants would sometimes have been allowed to seed themselves in the gravel if they could withstand

ABOVE: The herb garden at Fontevraud Abbey shows the geometric pattern of the traditional medieval garden.

being walked on. These could include thyme, pinks, violets, strawberries, and feverfew.

Stone paths were very unusual, but would have been made from flagstones or from tiles, or cobbles.

Flower Beds

The traditional picture is of raised beds, but if the drainage of the garden demanded it, the beds would be sunken. The important thing was that the beds and the paths should be of different heights to stop them from spreading into one another. However, raising the flower beds gives an exaggerated impression of the clean, geometric lines of the garden that are important to its symbolic meaning. The beds would be in simple, geometric shapes; generally squares although rectangles might be used, or squares with a corner or edge rounded to fit the overall design.

The edges of the beds would be held in place with low walls or fences of wattle, timber, stone, or tiles. The width of each bed would be the distance that a man could reach. This clearly had a practical function since it made it easier to tend the garden, but it also suited the principle that the garden was a piece of nature that had been tamed, simplified, and rendered controllable.

Flowers would usually have been planted singly in beds rather than in groups or drifts, although a particular plant might be used several times within the garden. Generally this gave a random effect within the flower beds, although sometimes certain features would be repeated regularly. For example, a rose might be planted at the inner corner of each of four central beds, or each border might have an iris at each end.

Sometimes even more order would be brought to the strictest gardens, taming nature even more dramatically. In these gardens, whole beds would be given over to one flower, or one plant would be grown at the back of a border with another all along the front. Perhaps foxgloves and irises along the back of the bed, fronted with columbines.

LEFT: The medieval garden was a microcosm of Paradise, a haven of recreation and good things.

THE ROMANCE OF THE ROSE

Gardens were often used in medieval literature as an allegorical representation of perfect love, or the fashionable "courtly love." These gardens were idealized, but were dream versions of the gardens of the time. *Le Roman de la rose*, or *The Romance of the Rose*, is one of the most famous of these verses. It was written in the thirteenth century and tells the story of a young hero who falls in love with a rosebud, and was so popular that Geoffrey Chaucer later translated it into English.

The Romance of the Rose was an allegorical warning of the dangers of improper love, in which the hero discovers a beautiful garden in a dream "by a castle wall hemmed round." The description of the garden is among the best contemporary accounts of the medieval garden that survives:

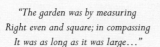

"The garden was by measuring
Right even and square; in compassing
It was as long as it was large…"

The poet tells of the clear wells and fountains in the gardens and, all around them:

"Sprang up the grass, as thick set
And soft as any velvet
On which man might his mistress lay
As on a feather bed to play
For the earth was soft and sweet
Through moisture of the well's wet."

The garden was so full of grace:

"That it of flowers had plenty
That both in summer and winter be
There sprang the violet all new
And fresh periwinkle rich of hue
And flowers yellow, white, and red,
More than ever grew in mead.
Joyous was the ground, and quaint
And spangled, as if it had been painted
With many a fresh and sundry flower
That offered up a sweet savor."

There are several gardens described in Giovanni Boccaccio's *Decameron*, written in the mid-fourteenth century. One of these is a walled garden with a lawn spangled with flowers, and a fountain at the center made of white marble, with a figure on the top from which the water spouted and then flowed away in channels.

The *Decameron* tells the story of a group of aristocrats fleeing from Florence to the surrounding hills to escape the plague. Having arrived in the town of Fiesole they rediscover the pleasures of civilized life, including the retreat of the walled garden, safe from the dangers of the city below.

GARDENS OF THE CLOISTERS
FORT TRYON PARK, NEW YORK, USA

These beautiful cloisters, three in all, are laid out according to simple ground plans. They are not strict re-creations of monastic cloisters since these would not have been planted up; they are secular cloisters, planted with flowers, shrubs, and trees typical of medieval European gardens. The Trie Cloister Garden is a copy (as far as possible) of the second of the Unicorn tapestries, which hangs in the museum at Fort Tryon. However, it includes flowers from all seven tapestries.

QUEEN ELEANOR'S GARDEN
WINCHESTER CASTLE, WINCHESTER, UK

This is a re-creation of a thirteenth-century castle garden in a small triangular space about 30 feet (10 m) by 100 feet (30 m). It is named after Queen Eleanor of Provence, wife of Henry III, and her daughter-in-law Queen Eleanor of Castile, who was married to Edward I. Its central feature is a fountain and water channel; the fountain column is modeled on a real one dating from the thirteenth century. It also contains a tunnel arbor, a turf seat, and a *hortus conclusus*, a small garden within the garden.

ABOVE: The private garden of a lady, from a fifteenth-century book of hours, with turf seats and white roses symbolizing virginity.

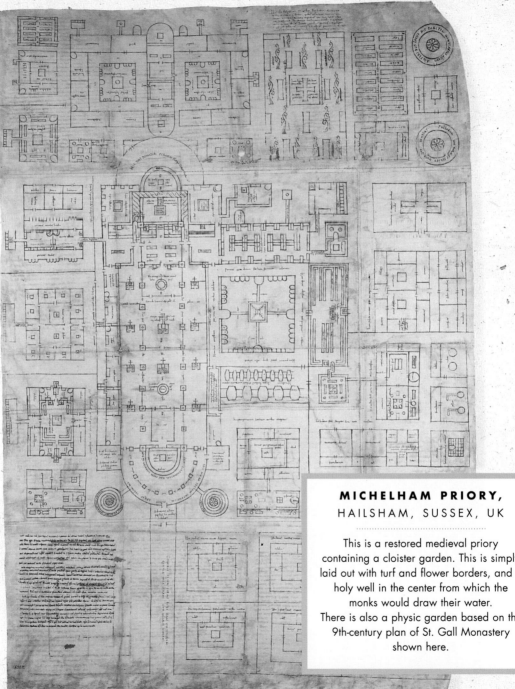

MICHELHAM PRIORY,
HAILSHAM, SUSSEX, UK

....

This is a restored medieval priory
containing a cloister garden. This is simply
laid out with turf and flower borders, and a
holy well in the center from which the
monks would draw their water.
There is also a physic garden based on the
9th-century plan of St. Gall Monastery
shown here.

Simplicity of Design

The design of the medieval gardens of Europe owes something to the gardens of Islam, which many European travelers had visited. The Christians, however, adapted the layout and incorporated their own style and religious symbolism to create a new kind of garden.

The medieval garden was surrounded by a wall or fence; the monks would have cloister gardens surrounded by a covered walkway. The garden within this enclosure would be divided by straight paths, often creating square beds or areas of turf. These geometric designs symbolized the taming of nature, since such patterns are not found in the natural, undomesticated landscape.

Sometimes the beds and turfed areas would be arranged in a checkerboard of squares, or the turf would be in the center of the garden surrounded by paths with a flower border around them. If there was a water source nearby, the center of the garden would be marked by a water feature. This would be a well, a pool, or a fountain. Sometimes the center of the garden would have a single tree planted in it, often the only tree in the garden.

Another popular feature of these gardens was the covered walkway, or tunnel arbor, which often separated different areas of the garden. This was usually covered with climbing roses, honeysuckle, or vines that filled in the sides as well as the top, although the plants were often trained so as to

create apertures like windows through which the garden could be viewed.

As well as the symbolism contained in the plants themselves, medieval garden owners would often include other features with strong symbolic overtones. The main turf of the garden might be divided into four squares to represent the four corners of the Earth. Or a vine might be planted over the entrance to symbolize the Tree of Life.

Arbors

Semicircular arbors made from coppiced poles were extremely popular and would be covered with vines, honeysuckle, or roses. Tunnel arbors were covered walkways made in the same way by bending wooden poles over a path to meet in the center. These tunnel arbors could have openings in the side as well as at each end. They were often planted with more than one climbing flower, for example, roses and honeysuckle together.

The arbor created an enclosed space within the already enclosed garden, and therefore represented the heart of the protected Heaven on Earth, and of the Virgin Mary herself.

Seats

Seating was most important and was always integral to the design of the garden, rather than bringing seats out from the house. This had two functions other than the purely practical: first, it allowed the garden to retain its simplicity of design, and second, it meant that the Paradise was complete – it needed no additions to enjoy it. Any time you entered the garden it was entire in itself and contained within its boundaries.

LEFT: This fifteenth-century illumination of a garden scene gives prominence to the fountain, a medieval symbol of the Trinity.

BELOW: The feeling of security from the evils of the world given by the walls of the medieval garden was an essential feature.

Seats were either made from earth mounds covered with turf, or from stone or timber filled with earth and then topped with turf. These seats could be hard to maintain in good condition, especially in dry weather, and they would often be returfed if a special guest was being entertained in the garden. Turf benches would either be straight or in a squared U-shape. Eating in the garden was popular. Tables were brought outside and placed in front of the permanent seats so they could be used at mealtimes.

THE FLOWERY MEAD

Many of the grassy areas in medieval gardens were full of flowers, as can be seen in many contemporary works of art. One of the most famous of these is a series of seven tapestries known as the Unicorn tapestries (which now hang in the Cloisters Museum in New York). These were embroidered as a wedding gift; the Unicorn symbolizes not only the bridegroom but also Christ. In the final tapestry it is tethered to a pomegranate tree within an enclosed garden; not only has the groom been captured and tethered to the tree of new life and fertility, but Christ has been enclosed by the Virgin Mary.

In and around the garden the turf is full of beautifully depicted flowers, including violas, carnations, campion, orchids, sweet rocket, lilies, holy thistle, leopard's bane, and lady's mantle. These all have symbolic interpretations.

Many of these flowery meads in medieval art were in fact drawn from wild habitats, but they were also incorporated into gardens. They were part way between a hay meadow and a piece of cultivated garden, and they would have been cut very low with a scythe, sometimes only twice a year. It can take years to develop a good hay meadow, so the best way to produce this kind of lawn is the same now as it was then: create a turfed area and cut holes in the turf into which the flowers can be planted individually. Suitable flowers include daisies, violets, periwinkle, primroses, cowslips, bluebells, wild strawberries, celandine, bugle, and eyebright.

Use slow-growing grass or it will quickly choke the flowers you have planted.

Turf

The art of creating a perfect lawn was as flourishing in the Middle Ages as it is now. Accounts survive of how to prepare a lawn. First the ground should be dug over and all roots and weeds removed. Then the whole area should be flooded with boiling water to kill any remaining seeds and pieces of root. Then the turf should be closely laid, and beaten down with mallets so that the joins can hardly be seen.

Cloister gardens usually contained only turf in the center, while noblemen's gardens might contain either turf or flower beds. For the monks, the color green was deeply symbolic, representing rebirth and eternal life. It was also thought to be the most restful color because it was halfway between black and white. One contemporary writer, Hugh of Fouilloy, wrote: "The green turf which is in the middle of the material cloister refreshes encloistered eyes and their desire to study returns. It is truly the nature of the color green that it nourishes the eyes and preserves their vision."

Outside the monasteries, however, many green turfs were allowed to fill up with flowers such as strawberries, violets, and daisies. When this practice was taken to extremes the lawn became known as a "flowery mead," consisting of more flowers than grass.

Fountains and Pools

Water was important in medieval gardens and was often used to create fountains where the supply was at a higher level than the garden. If necessary, a channel or stream would take the overflow of water away from the fountain pool. The design of fountains varied, but they were usually made from stone carved in the gothic style.

The fountain symbolized the trinity to the medieval Christians because it contains water in three different states: the bubbling up at the source or fountainhead, the sheet of water spilling into the pool, and the pool of still water at the base. Guillaume de Machaut wrote in praise of the Virgin Mary in the middle of the fourteenth century (trans. William Earle Nettles):

Three parts make up a fountain flow
The stream, the spout, the bowl.
Although these are three, these
three are one
Essence the same.
Even so the Waters of Salvation run.

Where it wasn't possible to create a fountain, the medieval garden would still have a pool. This would usually be lined with either lead or clay and have a stone surround. There would of course be nothing natural about its appearance: this was nature tamed and contained within an artificial design. Sometimes the pool would be still, but water channels would often flow in and out of this pool to keep the water moving and therefore ensuring it stayed clear.

Sometimes these pools contained fish, especially if they were in a monastery cloister. But in a nobleman's garden they were often used as small bathing or paddling pools, where gentlemen and ladies might dip their feet.

The Great Temptation

The gardens of the Middle Ages had an atmosphere of tranquillity rarely equaled in any other time. They achieved such success in creating a Heaven on Earth that at times they seemed to surpass Heaven itself; something that was seen as a temptation to the monks who tended their cloister gardens. It was dangerous to become too attached to your garden. One medieval writer told a cautionary tale of a monk who had reached the topmost rung on the ladder of virtue. But he looked down, and there he saw his own garden that he had created. Human desire overcame him and he toppled from his ladder because he chose the earthly Paradise over the heavenly one.

LEFT: Sculpture, like the surrounding architecture, is as much a part of this cloistered garden in New York City as the plants themselves.

CREATE YOUR OWN MEDIEVAL GARDEN

*I*f you are lucky enough to have a walled garden you can incorporate this design into it. If not, you can enclose the garden — or this section of it — with fencing or trellis. For a more authentic look than modern fencing, however, you could use wattle fencing. This comes in panels and is as straightforward to use as any other fencing, but it will need replacing every five to ten years.

This is a simple garden that could be a monastery cloister garden or a nobleman's garden.

KEY

1. Turf with daisies, violets, speedwell, and primroses in it

2. Gravel paths

3. Tunnel arbor with honeysuckle and roses climbing over it, and entrance onto central gravel path as well as at each end

4. Central pool with fountain (if water supply is difficult, this could be replaced with a single apple or mulberry tree)

5. Turf seats

FLOWER BEDS PLANTED WITH:

6. In a sunny aspect: roses, irises, white lilies, rosemary, sage, sweet rocket, yellow wallflower, fennel, holly hock, Verbascum (nigrum)

   In the shade: columbine, peony, lily-of-the-valley, roses, periwinkle, Solomon's seal, viola, feverfew, foxglove, woodruff, campion, hellebore

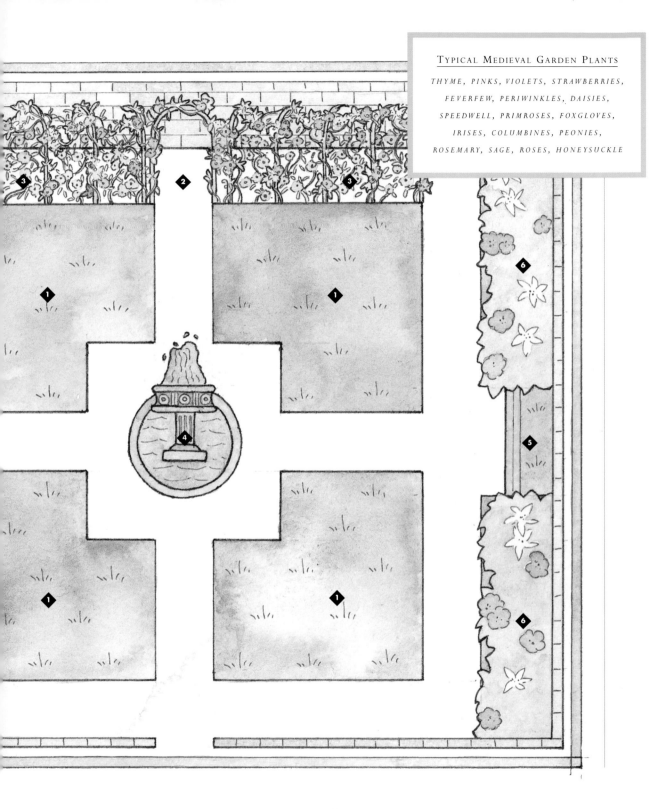

TYPICAL MEDIEVAL GARDEN PLANTS

THYME, PINKS, VIOLETS, STRAWBERRIES,
FEVERFEW, PERIWINKLES, DAISIES,
SPEEDWELL, PRIMROSES, FOXGLOVES,
IRISES, COLUMBINES, PEONIES,
ROSEMARY, SAGE, ROSES, HONEYSUCKLE

THE SHREWSBURY QUEST
SHREWSBURY, SHROPSHIRE, UK

This garden was laid out in 1994 as a re-creation of a monastic garden. The garden is contained within a cloister approximately 100 feet (30 m) square, divided into four sections. One of these quarters is set out as a green court, a simple turfed area with a tree in the center – a Glastonbury Thorn, said to be first planted by Joseph of Arimathea when he visited Glastonbury. He drove his staff into the ground and it sprouted; ever since then the thorn tree has flowered on Christmas Day.

The cloisters also include an Abbot's Herber, a classic four-square turf garden divided by paths with the abbey fish pond in the center and herb and flower borders around the edge. This is separated from the other sections of the garden by a tunnel arbor covered with roses, grapevines, and honeysuckle.

The remaining two sections of the garden are the physic garden, where the medicinal plants would have been grown, and the vegetable garden.

ABBAYE ROYALE
DE FONTEVRAUD
FONTEVRAUD, FRANCE

....

Fontevraud is the largest monastic city left in Europe, and the abbey itself consisted of four priories directed by nuns (the men who worked for them lived outside the enclosure). The abbey occupies 35 acres of land altogether, and includes an excellent re-creation of a monastic vegetable and herb garden. It also contains a cloister garden, simply turfed, with the turf divided by low hedges.

SIR ROGER VAUGHAN'S
GARDEN
TRETOWER COURT,
CRICKHOWELL, POWYS,
WALES

....

This garden, a re-creation of a fifteenth-century courtier's garden, incorporates a checkerboard layout of turf and flower beds, gravel paths, and diamond-patterned fencing. The central bed is a fountain in the form of a bowl dripping water from its edge into the pool beneath.
It also includes raised beds used as seats, and apple trees around the edge with tree seats, a popular medieval design. These involved making a raised bed about six feet (2 m) across, with a retaining fence or wall around them. The bed would be covered with turf for sitting on, and a standard tree planted in the center.

CHAPTER FIVE

ITALIAN RENAISSANCE GARDENS

As the Renaissance swept across Europe, the Italians applied their new view of the world to garden design. They drew on many older traditions — Roman, medieval, and Islamic — but their aim was to demonstrate humankind's supremacy over nature. They built gardens incorporating ordered patterns and a wealth of ornamental devices to amuse and impress visitors. The Renaissance gardens of Italy reflected the explosion of new thinking that began in fifteenth-century Europe.

According to the Book of Genesis, God gave humans dominion over nature, and Renaissance gardening in Italy was a celebration of God's gift. The wealthy inhabitants of Rome and Florence in the sixteenth century were steeped in Catholicism; arguably the first truly Renaissance garden was commissioned by Pope Julius II at the Villa Belvedere.

The Italians drew on a number of sources for their garden designs. From the medieval gardens they developed the idea of the garden as an outdoor room, linking many of these rooms together. They also took the medieval idea that straight lines and geometric shapes were important in a garden, as a symbol of order and control over the natural world.

BELOW: The glorious gardens of the Renaissance sprang from the rebirth of classicism. The palatial villas of sixteenth-century Italy set a style that was aspired to throughout Europe.

They often included a *giardino segreto,* or secret garden within their designs, echoing the *hortus conclusus* and also symbolizing Heaven on Earth.

The Italians were also acquainted with the Islamic gardens of Spain, Turkey, and the Near East, from which they took the symbolism and the esthetics of water. The water represented the four rivers that spring from beneath the Tree of Life in the Garden of Eden. However, the Italians stretched out one of the water channels — much as the Moguls had, and all but lost the channel that crossed it at right angles. Before long, this bisecting water channel became optional.

The other Islamic feature that was essential to the Renaissance garden was that of integrating the garden with the house. This had been achieved superbly by the Moors in Spain, and the Italians learned from them. However, they took it one step further and integrated the garden both with the house and with the landscape beyond. The view from their gardens looked over the outlying natural world that they had tamed and controlled, to emphasize the scale of their achievement.

The Gardens of Ancient Rome

The strongest influence, however, on the Renaissance gardens of Italy was the ancient Roman garden tradition. Although the Roman gardens were walled, they were sited on sloping ground so that they still had extensive views. They contained many buildings linking them to the house, or at least echoing it — colonnades, porticoes, courtyards, and trellises. They were also full of water features — fountains and water channels being especially popular.

One of the most sophisticated of all ancient Roman gardens was the one at Hadrian's Villa at Tivoli, the ruins of which still survive.

This included re-creations of famous buildings the emperor had visited, with pools and fountains. It was built on undulating ground, so that the hollows contained individual garden rooms, while the higher ground commanded views across the landscape beyond.

The Romans had a need to conquer and dominate land, which was echoed by their need to impose their will on their gardens. There was nothing natural here, but nature was overpowered by a huge array of architectural features and statues, grottoes, and topiary.

The Rebirth of Classical Gardening

The Italians took ideas from all three of these traditions and came up with a style of garden that was revolutionary, in a way that is almost impossible to appreciate now. Times had become a little more stable, so they no longer needed to surround their gardens with protective walls, and they took the opportunity to open them up on a grand scale.

The earliest garden that could be described as Renaissance was commissioned by Cosimo de' Medici in 1457, for his villa in Florence. The plants were used as a means of achieving the overall design more than as beautiful things in their own right. There was a strong emphasis on architecture in the garden, and the site made the most of the views across the countryside to the mountains.

However, the first pure Renaissance garden was built by Pope Julius II. It all began because he had a magnificent collection of antique sculptures that he wanted to display. He decided that they would look their best in an outdoor setting so he commissioned Donato Bramante to design a garden that would link his villa, the Villa Belvedere, to the Vatican palace. This would not only show off his sculptures, but should also provide a suitable setting for papal ceremonies. The two main challenges for the designer were that the villa and the palace were not quite in line with each other, and that the ground sloped from the palace up to the Villa Belvedere.

Bramante came up with a garden that not only fulfilled the brief but also demonstrated his complete control over nature. The most striking feature of this culmination of art over nature was symmetry in the garden. Bramante constructed a garden that contained loggias, symmetrical lawns on either side of a central axis, and a series of terraces carved out of the sloping ground. At the foot of the terraces was a huge open air theater, ideal for grand papal displays. It struck a chord in the people who visited it, that made them feel that they were leaving the Dark Ages behind and emerging into a world in which God allowed humans to control and order nature, with a confidence that was expressed in bold lines and wide open views.

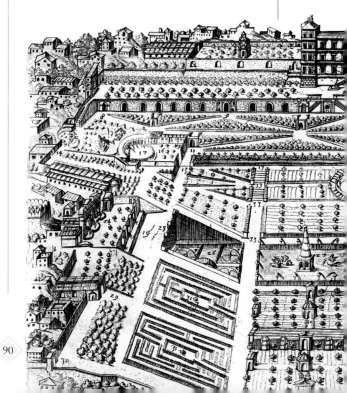

RIGHT: A water staircase, as at the Villa Cicogna near Lake Lugano, was another possibility for a grand garden on a sloping site. Trees and shrubs and their strong shadows in the bright light form part of the design.

The Hillside Setting

Much of the Italian landscape is hilly, and around Florence and Rome – the two cities at the forefront of garden fashion – it became essential to build your Renaissance garden on the hillside. The idea was to have the garden running up the hillside from the villa in a series of terraces, so that it could be viewed from the house as it rose up above it.

Water would run down through the garden from a source at the top, creating the central axis of the garden. The terraces would contain many architectural features – extensions of the house – such as loggias, pavilions, colonnades, and fountains, all with classical Roman overtones. There would generally be a dominant feature at the top of the garden, and another showpiece at the bottom where the water channel or cascade finished near the villa. It was intended that either of these could be seen as the main feature of the garden, so that whichever end of the garden you stood at, the whole was in balance.

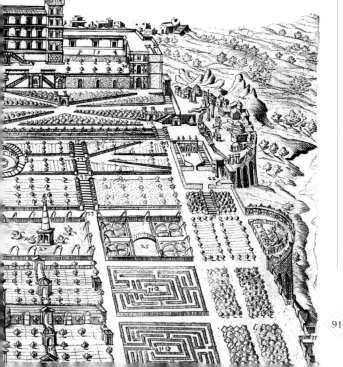

To create a garden on a hillside required more skill, more artistic challenge, and more sheer disruption of the natural landscape than gardening on flat ground. So it was a greater triumph of art over nature. The Renaissance garden was all about cultivating and creating life, which was considered to be ordered by God; not only could the garden builders control nature in imitation of God's power, they could improve on it.

LEFT: The sloping sides of Italian gardens offered the possibility of tiered terraces and spectacular water displays. The Villa d'Este had literally hundreds of fountains in its formal terraces.

Alberti's Principles of Design

Leon Battista Alberti was an architect who lived in fifteenth-century Florence. He was also a scholar of the classical tradition, and he took many of his ideas from the writings of the ancient Romans. One of his central themes was that each section of the garden must be seen in terms of its proportion to the whole; this classical theory of proportion led to garden architects laying out gardens on a grand scale with the emphasis on the overall effect first, and the detail second.

The most extreme expression of control over nature was symmetry. Alberti wrote that laurels, cedars, and junipers should be planted, often intertwined, but in rows set out evenly, with pairs of exactly opposite trees in perfectly straight lines. Box hedges and myrtles could also be set out either side of the walks and used to create parterres on the lower slopes that could be viewed from the windows of the house.

Many of these trees had symbolic meanings. The laurel was popular with the ancient Romans and symbolized victory. It was thought to be spiritually cleansing. The laurel wreath symbolized poetry to the Romans, and artistic excellence, both associations the Renaissance designers wanted to incorporate into their gardens. The Romans held myrtle to be sacred to Venus, and since the new gardens were intended as places of pleasure, relaxation, and amorous pursuits – rather than the protective sanctuaries they used to be – this also suited very well.

Alberti also urged garden designers to include architectural features in their gardens, as the Romans had. As time went on these became more ornate and included statues of classical subjects, often mythological, and grottoes, labyrinths, and other elaborate features.

BELOW: Strategically placed basins, fountains, and trees not only add the elements of cool water and green shade, but also introduce scale.

VILLA LANTE, BAGNAIA

This garden, begun in 1566, is one of the most beautiful of all Renaissance gardens. It is smaller and simpler than many, and it balances nature and architecture perfectly. The villa itself, at the bottom of the slopes, has been split into two, framing the view of the central water axis. The surrounding woods encroach closer around the sides than in any previous Renaissance garden, highlighting the contrast. (By the end of the sixteenth century the Baroque style brought the surrounding wild woods right into gardens.)

The water parterre by the house contains a beautiful fountain and stone boats "floating" in the pools around it. Higher up the garden, the water spouts from fountains, foams down channels, cascades over waterfalls, and even forms a pool in the center of an outdoor stone dining table for cooling the wine.

At the top of the garden the spring rises between pavilions where paths disappear into the surrounding woods. The message of the garden is that there is a balance between the wildness of the woods at the top and the ordered control of the parterre at the bottom; both are linked by the water that connects them.

BELOW: *The tranquil formal pool or water parterre at the Villa Lante is ornamented by an elaborate fountain and stone boats, set off by carefully arranged stone urns.*

BELOW: The tranquil formal pool or water parterre at the Villa Lante is ornamented by an elaborate fountain and stone boats, set off by carefully arranged stone urns.

PALAZZO FARNESE,
CAPRAROLA

The Farnese gardens outside Rome are split into two parts, separated by woods. In the most famous of these, the path leads unexpectedly to a grass avenue flanked by pine trees, with a view up through cascades and a "water chain" – a stone-carved chain with water flowing down along it – to a pavilion, beyond which is a *giardino segreto,* or secret garden, watched over by statues on three sides.

The gardens as a whole are classic Renaissance gardens, built on a hillside and occupying a pentagonal-shaped site with plantations of trees as well as the two gardens.

BOBOLI GARDENS
PITTI PALACE, FLORENCE

This garden was begun in 1550 and was built for Cosimo de' Medici; it is beautifully illustrated in one of the *Utens Lunettes,* a series of 14 paintings each depicting one of the Medici gardens around Florence. The Boboli Gardens were laid out behind the Pitti Palace and contain a horseshoe-shaped amphitheater, thickly planted with trees in the steepest part except along the central axis that remains open, leading the eye upward along it. Since the area immediately behind the house was used in this way, the parterre was, unusually, laid out at the side of the house instead.

THE COMPONENTS OF THE ITALIAN RENAISSANCE GARDEN

Borders

Usually the perimeter of the garden was marked with walls covered with plants; this gave the impression of controlled nature far better than bare walls. The plants were trained on trellis or wooden laths, and the most common climbers were ivy and vines. Fruit trees were also sometimes trained on the walls, their naturally three-dimensional shapes trained into two-dimensional ones with straight espaliered branches.

Sometimes the garden would be bounded by a hedge of some kind, usually evergreen but sometimes of fruit trees. The smaller garden rooms within the outer perimeter were often marked with lower hedges of myrtle, lavender, box, or rosemary, often mixed together. Sometimes these sections of the garden would be separated by avenues of trees. Once a landscape was terraced, retaining walls were created to hold the terraces back. These walls were often covered with espaliered citrus or pomegranate trees.

Water

Water is essential to the Renaissance garden, both literally and metaphorically. The central axis of the garden contains a flow of water, running along channels, through fountains, down cascades, opening into still pools or rippling through little stone-edged streams. Water is always there in one form or another.

As you stand at the bottom of the terraces by the villa, the eye is drawn up the hillside by the water. The main axis of the garden would have a number of smaller garden rooms opening off it, and these would frequently be centered on their own water feature. This could be a pool, a fountain or even an amusing water device to trick visitors into getting a soaking. To control water is the ultimate expression of power over nature, since water is such a capricious element to tame. So not only was the water cool and refreshing, and a source of constant movement in the garden, it also symbolized the architect's art in its highest form.

Parterres

The terrace nearest the house – which was almost always at the bottom of the hillside rather than the top – was laid out in parterres designed to be viewed from the upper windows of the house. These intricate patterns were laid out in low hedges, often of box, which were usually filled in with flowers. The patterns tended to be geometric, although later they developed into more intricate designs, such as a copy of the family's coat of arms. Initially, circles and squares were the most popular shapes, since – as in Islamic design – these represented the meeting of matter and spirit (the yin and yang of Taoist and Zen gardens) and represented divine inspiration in the art that controlled nature.

Renaissance gardens were far more flower-filled and colorful when they were first made than the surviving ones tend to be now. The parterres were often filled with colorful flowers: irises, carnations, hollyhocks, lilies, poppies, primroses, pansies, narcissi, hyacinths, and many others.

A water parterre was one that included pools as well as flower beds in the overall design, often with fountains featured in the middle of the pool. The clipped hedges and the water would integrate to form the overall design.

RIGHT: The Dragon Fountain provides one of the many architectonic water displays at the Villa d'Este (Tivoli).

WATER DEVICES

One of the most popular features of Renaissance gardens was known as *giochi d'acqua*, or water tricks. These were not only highly fashionable, but also took the whole idea of controlling the garden to a new level. Water, a natural element, could not only be tamed, but could even be laughed at.

Water tricks came in all sorts of guises. One of the most popular was to conceal a mechanism that would be inadvertently tripped by visitors, turning a peaceful area of the garden into a fountain of water jets that would drench them. Statues would emit water from nostrils and ears, and some were designed to be either erotic or obscene. In the garden at Villa Castello near Florence there was a fountain designed as a rock surmounted by a copper medallion. This bears the form of a very old man sitting down. Water is dripping slowly from his beard, forehead, and skin, representing sweat and tears.

The Villa d'Este at Tivoli, near Rome, is the ultimate Renaissance garden, full of such water features. The Owl Fountain is a statue of a group of birds that are made to sing by means of water pressure and fall silent whenever a mechanical owl turns to face them.

Also at the Villa d'Este is the Organ Fountain. Large tanks filled up with water from the river to provide pressure. This pressure built up in the air in a vaulted recess, and also drove a wheel with teeth that hit a keyboard. This supposedly imitated a range of sounds including organs, cannon, and trumpets.

ABOVE: The Boboli Gardens in Florence,
showing the essential features of a Renaissance garden.

Flowers

The flowers mentioned above and others were
grown in different parts of the garden in urns and
in flower beds. They were always planted in an
ordered fashion, never in a naturalistic way. Beds
would contain one or two flowers in blocks,
perhaps bordered by another variety.

Many summer flowering annual flowers were
grown, such as nasturtiums and *Impatiens balsamifera*,
which would be bedded out when the bulbs were
lifted. Roses and jasmine were commonly grown
over pergolas and arbors for their beautiful scent as
much as for their color.

Living Tunnels

Another survivor from the medieval garden was the
tunnel arbor. The Italians, with their hot climate,
loved to build tunnels, pergolas, and colonnades
covered with climbing plants — ivy, vines, jasmine,
and roses — to shade them from the sun. In the
Moorish gardens of Spain, the brightness of the
courtyard gardens as you emerged from the
darkness of the buildings symbolized the soul
emerging into Paradise. The Renaissance tunnel
arbors also represented the dawn of the new age.

A pergola or tunnel often ran along the back of
the parterre, leading to the rest of the garden. This

might be made of living trees trained to twine together, or of lattice or bent stakes over which climbers were grown. Sometimes these incorporated domes, doorways, and windows, all in classical style. Or stone colonnades, often roofed with tiles, would be constructed and covered with climbing plants. The heat of the Italian summers made such shady walkways very welcome features.

Statues

All good classical gardens contained statues, so the Renaissance garden designers did the same. Many of these took classical subjects, and since water was such a key feature, many statues were of water nymphs and gods.

Other features also took classical themes; the parkland beside the formal gardens at the Villa Lante north of Rome included an entire hillside to represent Mount Parnassus, the mythical home of the Greek muses. Here the theme was not water deities but classical figures of artistic inspiration, equally appropriate to the cultured Renaissance garden.

The Space Beyond

The land and the views beyond the formal, ordered garden were as essential as the garden itself; in a sense they were part of it. The balance between art and nature had to be struck, and with little room for nature within the garden, it had to be found beyond its borders.

The view of meadows and woods beyond the garden was of such importance that, if these features didn't actually exist, they had to be planted. This time the plantings were as natural as possible, so as to offer a striking contrast with the straight lines and subjugation of nature within the garden.

BELOW: Renaissance garden statues were often of water or nature gods.

CREATE YOUR OWN
ITALIAN RENAISSANCE GARDEN

Unless you have a substantial amount of land it is impossible even to attempt to re-create a classic Renaissance garden. However, it is perfectly possible to create a garden in the style of one of the garden rooms in a Tuscan villa. If there are attractive views beyond the boundary, you can open up a section of the wall or hedge to reveal them.

You can always build the façade of a classical summerhouse against the back wall rather than the full structure, if space is limited.

This type of garden calls for plenty of maintenance, especially clipping the box hedges, so be prepared for this before you build it.

TYPICAL RENAISSANCE
GARDEN PLANTS

IVY, VINES, FRUIT TREES, LAUREL, MYRTLE, LAVENDER, BOX, ROSEMARY, IRISES, CARNATIONS, HOLLYHOCKS, LILIES, POPPIES, PRIMROSES, PANSIES, NARCISSUS, HYACINTHS, ROSES, JASMINE

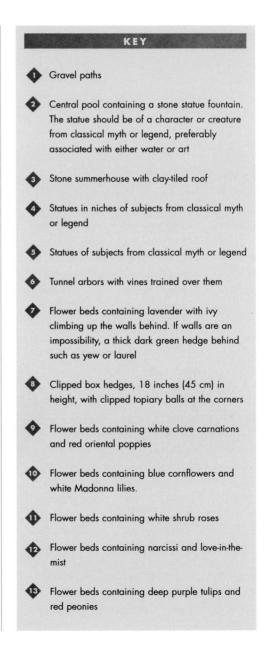

KEY

1. Gravel paths

2. Central pool containing a stone statue fountain. The statue should be of a character or creature from classical myth or legend, preferably associated with either water or art

3. Stone summerhouse with clay-tiled roof

4. Statues in niches of subjects from classical myth or legend

5. Statues of subjects from classical myth or legend

6. Tunnel arbors with vines trained over them

7. Flower beds containing lavender with ivy climbing up the walls behind. If walls are an impossibility, a thick dark green hedge behind such as yew or laurel

8. Clipped box hedges, 18 inches (45 cm) in height, with clipped topiary balls at the corners

9. Flower beds containing white clove carnations and red oriental poppies

10. Flower beds containing blue cornflowers and white Madonna lilies.

11. Flower beds containing white shrub roses

12. Flower beds containing narcissi and love-in-the-mist

13. Flower beds containing deep purple tulips and red peonies

Tuscan Gardens

Although many of the gardens around Florence were laid out in classic Renaissance style, there were still a number of Tuscans who resisted the change to some extent. Perhaps because of the intimacy of their landscape they preferred to keep their gardens closer to the medieval style, but with many Renaissance influences.

The very earliest Renaissance garden – the one built for Cosimo de' Medici at the Villa Careggi – was an example of this style, and many Tuscan garden designers chose not to develop the Renaissance theme further. These gardens did not necessarily include water features, certainly not in the way that the great Renaissance gardens did. They retained a series of medieval-style garden rooms, although these were more likely to be influenced by the Renaissance style in being stretched along a central axis. They added statues and perhaps a grotto or a fountain, or opened up a view, but essentially they retained the secret feel of the earlier gardens.

Small garden enclosures with high walls would be planted with simply designed parterres or beds edged with clipped box; these would often have a tunnel walkway right around the edge. The garden was not necessarily integrated with the house, in terms either of proportion or of spilling the house into the garden in pavilions, loggias, and other indoor-outdoor buildings.

However, these were Renaissance gardens. Symmetry became more dominant, with avenues of trees and bushes, often along the central line, and vases and statues decorating the garden.

At the other end of the scale, however, many of the greatest examples of Renaissance gardens were also created in Tuscany, in the hills around Florence. The most notable of these were the Boboli gardens at the Pitti Palace in Florence.

LEFT: Gardens such as those of the Villa Careggi (from the fifteenth century) are less grandiose and vaunting than the later Renaissance gardens, although they share such features as formality and symmetry of design with them. The wisteria rambling against the mellow walls of the villa has a softening naturalistic effect.

VILLA D'ESTE
TIVOLI

....

This garden is thought to be the most spectacular of all Renaissance gardens, and the one that uses water most dominantly and to greatest effect. It was built between 1550 and 1580. Although the villa is at the top of the hill, the entrance to the garden was originally at the bottom and the route to the villa led up a grand axial stairway through terraces, cascades, fountains, and water features, to the house and a stunning view of the countryside.

The garden contained many elaborate water games and statues, often pillaged from Hadrian's Villa, which is nearby, many of which have since disappeared. There were grottoes with imitation seaweed, water staircases, and fountains to produce mist or rainbow effects.

Although the *giochi d'acqua* no longer functions, the fountains and streams are as enchanting as ever, the most famous of all being the Walk of a Hundred Fountains. This is a walk edged on one side by three terraced rows of small fountains, each playing into its own water channel. Between the fountains are stucco reliefs depicting scenes from Ovid's *Metamorphoses*, a collection of legends and fables about mythical transformations, echoing the transformation of nature to art within the garden.

CHAPTER SIX

ENGLISH KNOT GARDENS

*T*he Italian fashion
for parterres — intricate
designs in low-cut hedges designed to
be viewed from above — spread north into
Europe. By the time it reached England it had
developed into the knot garden, a complicated design of low
hedges intertwined, which symbolized the journey of life
or, sometimes, the partnership of marriage. Knot
gardens might be garden rooms in their own
right, but they were often laid out as
part of a larger garden
design.

At the end of the fifteenth century the Italian influence on garden design began to spread, notably to France where they began to develop huge vista gardens. The most fashionable Italian gardens had been situated on hillsides, but the French began to develop their gardens on the plains of northern France where everything could be seen in a single sweep from the château. The main ingredient in these French gardens was the parterre, always made from box and designed to be viewed from the upstairs windows of the house since the formal reception rooms of the time were upstairs.

LEFT: The seventeenth-century knot
garden at Hampton Court Palace
(England) has a cheerful intimacy.

Italian parterres had been geometric in design, but
the French developed complex patterns that
resembled the embroidery of the new silks being
imported from India, so the designs became known
as *broderie*. The box hedges might be interplanted
with flowers, but often the pattern was made to
stand out by infilling the hedges with distinctive
colors such as brick dust, crushed coal, marble,
shells, or sand. The parterre was an expression,
as it had been in Italy, for humankind's dominion
over the natural world.

The English Style

The fashion for parterres reached as far as England
in the sixteenth and seventeenth centuries, but the
English reinterpreted the style to create knot
gardens. A very simple form of these had already
been developed as an extension of medieval garden
design. Knot gardens were also created on the
European continent, in particular in France and
Holland, but the knot garden became especially
associated with English gardens. By the end of the
sixteenth century no self-respecting manor house
could be without one.

The knot garden differed from the parterre not
only in being smaller, but also in style. It was
constructed with a square outline, reminiscent of
the medieval gardens that it superseded. The square
symbolizes humanity, and the knot garden – like the
medieval garden – is a celebration of humanity.

The English knot garden still retained many
elements of the parterre. It was outlined in low
hedges that might be infilled with gravel or sand,
perhaps with a specimen plant in each segment, or
completely filled with plants, with one or more
varieties to a section. These were called open knots.
A closed knot was planted with the hedges so close
together that there were barely any spaces in

ABOVE: Patience is needed in creating a knot garden,
as the intricate framework for the garden consists of
living shrubs which knit together as they grow.

between. Topiary balls or simple shapes were
sometimes incorporated into the hedges, and the
center of the knot might feature a clipped box, bay,
or juniper tree, an upright rosemary bush, or an
apothecary's rose *(Rosa gallica officinalis)*.

Like the parterre, the knot garden was intended
to be viewed from above. It could be constructed
very quickly if necessary, and there are accounts of
knot gardens being created in time for royal visits,
sited below the window of the royal visitor's
sleeping chamber.

Another feature that parterres and knots shared
was the inspiration for their designs. Early knots
were based on simple squares and circles, but later
on, by the seventeenth century, they took their
ideas from the *broderie* style. They also took patterns
from wooden carvings or plasterwork inside the
house, or from the owners' initials or coat of arms.

RIGHT: In the early knot gardens the areas
between the evergreen "threads" were generally
filled with gravel or other colored stone. This
example at Hatfield House (England) dates
from the early seventeenth century.

The Symbolism of Knots

Knot gardens are invariably designed in the shape of
an endless knot; that is to say, there are no ends to
the design but the pattern can be followed around
continuously. This represents infinity, since it has no
beginning and no end. It also symbolizes the "knot
of destiny," the tortuous path from which only
Christ can free the human soul. So the knot garden
is a positive symbol of the eternal life of the soul;
the line of the hedges traces the journey of the soul.

The changing seasons in the garden were viewed
as a symbol of the pattern of human life – birth,
life, death, and rebirth. To the Christians, this
rebirth was of course a rebirth to a new life in
Heaven, but this view of gardens is far older and
also draws on the pagan idea of being forever
reborn to a succession of lives on Earth. However,
the knot garden all but defies this symbolism, since
it barely changes from season to season – its
structure is constant and it is usually planted in
evergreen plants. So it represents the power of the
soul live eternally.

There were other symbolisms often employed in
knot gardens. One is the idea that a knot is
something that binds two things together. Knot
gardens were often designed as lovers' knots,
perhaps intertwining two sets of initials. Also, knots
were traditionally worn in clothes to ward off evil,
since they bind up the evil spirit and render it
powerless, and knot gardens therefore gave
protection to the houses they were attached to.

In order to emphasize the impression that the
hedges were creating a knotted pattern, it became
fashionable to give the appearance that the hedges
wove under and over each other. This was done by
using more than one plant (and therefore more than
one shade of green) to make the hedges. At the
points where they crossed, one was cut slightly
lower than the one that passed through it, making it
seem to thread underneath it.

ABOVE: A true knot garden is based
on the design of a continuous,
flowing thread, symbolizing our
journey through life.

THE COMPONENTS OF THE ENGLISH KNOT GARDEN

The Site and Shape

Knot gardens were constructed on level ground and in view of the upper windows of the house, from where the pattern could best be seen. Occasionally the knot would be rectangular but more often it would be square. It frequently echoed the design of medieval gardens by being made in a square intersected by crossing paths, creating four smaller squares. These would normally all follow the same design, since knot gardens are traditionally symmetrical. Where the paths crossed in the center, the center point would normally be marked with a fountain or pool (representing the water of life), or with a sundial (symbolizing how human life – represented by the knot itself – is bound by time), or some other feature such as a clipped bay tree or a rose bush.

Borders

The knot is usually – though not always – surrounded by a square hedge that runs all the way around it. This was often surrounded by a low rail about half the height of the hedge and made of hard wood such as elm, which might be either painted or left bare. This served to protect the plants from children or dogs, and also from being brushed by the long dresses and cloaks of the time.

The rail also had another function. It enclosed the knot and created a garden that was not to be entered; this indicated that the symbolic power of the knot should not be broken.

Hedges

The hedges of the knot garden should be low, but there is no specific height. They are not generally above two feet (60 cm), but they may be as little as six inches (15 cm) or even less. Originally only one kind of plant was used, usually box, lavender, rosemary, santolina (cotton lavender), or wall germander. For purely practical reasons, it is necessary to be able to step over the hedges to tend the center of the garden, since there are no paths.

By the seventeenth century, as designs became more ambitious, other plants were also used, such as hyssop, winter savory, thyme, and southernwood. Some of these are less reliable in cold winters because they may lose some of their leaves.

Some of these plants come in more than one color – for example there are both silver and green santolinas – and these were ideal for winding in and out of one another. Although the knot designs could

BELOW: *Some of the most successful knot gardens are achieved with just one hedging plant. In northern climates, grass can be used for the pathways to create a restful composition all in green.*

be very complex, the planting tended to be fairly simple – so as not to detract from the design. So only three or four hedging plants at the most would be used in a closed knot, and perhaps only one or two in an open knot, with maybe another color for the square border hedge. It also continued to be popular to use one hedging plant only, except for lovers' knots, which tended to require two colors, and perhaps a third for the edging.

Infill

If the knot is filled in with gravel, sand, or chippings, it can be more complex in design and

Some of the most successful knot gardens are achieved with just one hedging plant. In northern climates, grass can be used for the pathways to create a restful composition all in green.

still retain a strong shape. Two or three different colored materials can be used to fill in the spaces, for example red brick dust, crushed coal, or white sand or shells.

The alternative way to fill in the spaces is with flowers. These can either be grouped *en masse* in each space, or a selection can be planted in each gap. The classic knot garden would have had a single species to each gap, often repeated within the overall pattern, to make the design stand out better.

Another option, as a halfway point, was to fill the spaces with gravel or sand and then plant a single specimen flower in the center of each space, or the larger spaces. This could either be planted directly in the ground, or it could be planted in a pot and placed in position.

Flowers

The type of flowers used for knot gardens would be related to the height of the hedges. The flowers should not be lower than the surrounding hedges, so if low-growing plants were used, the hedges would be clipped shorter. Lots of short plants were popular according to contemporary reports of knot gardens, so presumably the hedges were often kept low. These lower plants include primroses, violets, heartsease (wild pansies), double daisies, periwinkle, and auriculas. Since these are largely spring flowers, the knot would have been almost entirely green for most of the summer and fall.

The most popular taller plants for knot gardens were marigolds, cornflowers, columbines, pinks, rue, sage, and marjoram.

The use of flowers had developed a language of its own by Tudor times, and the flowers that were planted often had deliberate meanings. The colors of flowers largely determined their message; the following list indicates their meanings:

   RED   *Passion, love, blood*
   YELLOW   *Royalty*
   BLUE   *Happiness*
   GREEN   *Remembrance*
   PINK   *Contentment, peacefulness*
   WHITE   *Purity*

Other types of flowers had other meanings, not all so pleasant. Thorny plants, for example, represented pain, and weeds symbolized vices.

This meant that knot gardens could be planted with flowers that all reinforced a particular symbolism. A lovers' knot, of intertwining hedges, could contain entirely flowers that symbolized love in some way. For example, red and white carnations or pinks, blue hyacinths, and veronica for love; white lilies for purity; blue Canterbury bells for faithfulness; and a clipped bay tree in the center to symbolize immortality.

A garden could equally well be planted to symbolize religious piety. This could contain violets for humility, double daisies and wild strawberries for innocence, clove pink *(Dianthus caryophyllus)* for the soul, sweet marjoram for virtue, rue for repentance, and white lilies for the Virgin Mary.

One of the best examples of a knot garden was laid out in the early part of this century on the site of Shakespeare's house in Stratford-upon-Avon in Warwickshire, England. Shakespeare would have been very familiar with knot gardens and with the meanings of the flowers within them; in *Hamlet*, Ophelia, having gone mad, presents flowers to her brother and the king and queen saying:

"There's rosemary, that's for remembrance… And there is pansies, that's for thoughts. There's fennel for you, and columbines. There's rue for you, and here's some for me. We may call it herb of grace o' Sundays."

MAZES AND LABYRINTHS

Mazes and labyrinths had developed in Italy and France alongside parterres and attained popularity in England at the same time as knot gardens. The English planted them in gardens as a variation on knot gardens, although a garden might well contain both.

The terms "maze" and "labyrinth" mean virtually the same thing in garden terms, although mazes tend to imply a puzzle in which the challenge is to reach a particular point – usually the center (by a multicursal path that divides and confuses the follower). A labyrinth is a regular shape, generally a variation on the spiral, which simply has to be followed to reach the center (a unicursal path). The original labyrinth was constructed at Knossos in Crete and was supposedly built to contain the Minotaur, half-man, half-bull, in its center.

In Christian times, however, the labyrinth became a symbol of the tortuous journey of the soul as it wove its way through life, or the journey from darkness into light. While many mazes and labyrinths were also built for fun, the people of Tudor England would have been well aware of their deeper meaning.

The multicursal mazes represented the distractions and sidetracks tempting the soul from the path of true belief. In the sixteenth century this type of maze would have been about knee-height, but by the seventeenth century they were made with towering hedges so that followers could not even see their goal. Once the hedges became taller they were often used by lovers who would enter the maze separately and then try to find each other.

Maze hedges were usually made from dense-growing plants, such as box or yew, but they could also be made from trellis planted with climbers that would create a reasonably thick cover – such as honeysuckle – so that you might see through the trellis beside you, but you wouldn't be able to see through the one beyond it.

The unicursal maze is a very ancient pattern. There is one carved into the rock in Sardinia, which is 4,000 years old. The earliest mazes often had seven rings in the spiral, but the Christian Church introduced the 11-ring maze, representing the 11 true apostles. These mazes or labyrinths symbolized the hazardous pilgrim's path to Jerusalem and the Crusades, and were often incorporated into church design. The most famous is made from blue and white marble set into the floor of Chartres cathedral.

In gardens, these mazes would have been made by cutting turf to create paths between the grass. They were walked, from the entrance to the center, as a meditation. They could also be followed on the knees as an act of penitence. Labyrinths can trace an extremely long route without occupying a great deal of space. The one in Chartres cathedral, for example, is only 40 feet (12 m) across, but the path it follows is almost an eighth of a mile (200 m) long.

LEFT: A maze such as this is of very ancient design.

The Development of Plant Symbolism

Flowers and plants have carried hidden meanings for people in all cultures. The Greeks and Romans named many flowers after gods and goddesses or heroes and created stories around them. Narcissus was a beautiful young man who fell in love with his own reflection in a pool of water. Reaching out to touch it, he fell in and drowned and was turned into a flower.

By medieval times, the symbolism of plants in Europe had become Christian. So the lily, which had been sacred to the Greek mother goddess Hera (Juno to the Romans) became sacred to the Virgin Mary. The rose was revered by the Greeks and Romans as being sacred to the goddess of love, Aphrodite (Venus); it was also a funereal flower because of the painful associations of its thorns. By medieval times it had become sacred to the Christians and represented the blood of Christ – the thorns symbolized his suffering.

In Tudor times the symbolism shifted again, and flowers largely came to be associated with human characteristics. So the white lily became a symbol of purity, although its association with the Virgin Mary was not forgotten. And the rose became the symbol of love, while its thorns symbolized the pain of human passion.

Other flowers in Tudor times represented human characteristics such as eloquence (sweetly scented flowers), flattery (fennel), binding affection (honeysuckle), passion (mulberry), and nostalgia (heartsease). While some individual flowers had their own meanings, all flowers would be classified symbolically by color or type.

RIGHT: Many of the plants grown in the gardens of the past were imbued with symbolic value, although their symbolism sometimes changes with time.

LILY

HONEYSUCKLE

ROSE

THE TUDOR GARDEN
SOUTHAMPTON, HAMPSHIRE, UK

There are no original knot gardens left in England – most of them were cleared to make way for the later fashion for landscape gardening. But this garden is attached to a Tudor house and is made as a representation of a garden of the time. It is not large enough for an exact replica garden, but it features examples of the gardens of the time – a tunnel arbor, a fountain, and so on. It also includes a knot garden, the design of which is taken from books of garden patterns dating from the sixteenth century. This is made from hedges of box, santolina, wall germander, and winter savory, infilled with gravel and specimen plants.

NEW PLACE GARDEN
STRATFORD-UPON-AVON, UK

This is a very mature knot garden, having been planted in 1919, long before the fashion for re-creating gardens of the Tudor period. It is part of a larger Elizabethan garden that includes an excellent example of a tunnel arbor, also re-created, and the original orchard and kitchen garden of the house, New Place, which belonged to William Shakespeare. The knot garden is made on the site of the original house (which is no longer standing).

This is a quadripartite knot garden; it is square and divided by stone paths into four separate knots. The ornate designs for these knots – each one different – are taken from garden books of the early seventeenth century. As recommended in these books, the hedges are made from box, savory, hyssop, cotton lavender, and thyme, and the spaces are filled in with blocks of flowers in bright colors.

ABOVE: The Tudor Garden in Southampton (England) features a reproduction knot garden.

CREATE YOUR OWN
KNOT GARDEN

English knot gardens were at their most popular in the sixteenth and seventeenth centuries. As time went on, the designs became more complicated, but early designs were based on simple circles and squares, such as this one. This design includes under-and-over hedges, and also happens to be in the shape of an ancient Celtic symbol known as the triple enclosure. It represents the human mind: the outer square is the conscious mind that takes in the world through the five senses; the central square is the spiritual mind or soul; and the square between is receptive to both God and the outside world. The knot garden is planted with flowers that reinforce this symbolism.

KEY	
1	Box hedge two feet (60 cm) high
2	Santolina (cotton lavender) hedge two feet (60 cm) high
3	Lavender *(Lavandula angustifolia)* – grown to ease the mind , to symbolize consciousness
4	Lavender and opium poppies *(Papaver somniferum)* – to symbolize consciousness and sleep
5	Clove pink *(Dianthus caryophyllus)* to symbolize the soul
6	Clove pink and opium poppies – to symbolize the soul and sleep

TYPICAL KNOT GARDEN PLANTS

BOX, LAVENDER, ROSEMARY, SANTOLINA, PRIMROSES, VIOLETS, HEARTSEASE, DOUBLE DAISIES, PERIWINKLES, MARIGOLDS, CORNFLOWERS, COLUMBINES, PINKS, RUE, SAGE, MARJORAM, CARNATIONS, LILIES, BAY TREE, JUNIPER TREE

RED LODGE GARDEN, RED LODGE MUSEUM, BRISTOL, UK

The Red Lodge is a Tudor building dating from the end of the sixteenth century and is now a museum of the period. In 1980, it was decided that a period house should have a period garden to go with it. The garden is not normally open to the public, so it needed to be of a design that could be appreciated from the upper windows of the house; for this reason they decided to create a knot garden with a surrounding path and flower beds.

The design for the knot was taken, from the plasterwork design on one of the ceilings on the first floor of the house. The outline of the knot is in box, and the spaces between the hedges are filled with rue, purple-leaved sage, and colored gravel.

LITTLE MORETON HALL CHESHIRE, UK

This house is a perfect example of a timber-framed moated manor house with a Tudor garden surrounding it. The knot garden is based on a design in *The English Gardener* published in 1670, although the design itself probably dates from the late sixteenth century. It is an open knot of box hedging infilled with gravel. At each end of the knot garden itself are borders, planted in a regular pattern and also surrounded by low box hedging that contain flowering plants of the period.

These include standard gooseberries clipped into balls and underplanted with irises, peonies, crane's-bills, perennial flax, thrift, and herbs.

PETERSFIELD PHYSIC GARDEN
PETERSFIELD, HAMPSHIRE, UK

This garden is set in an ancient walled burgage plot (an area of land rented out at a fixed rate) behind a house in Petersfield High Street. Although small, the garden is planted exactly as it might have been in the seventeenth century, after the style of a famous botanist of the period, John Goodyer, who lived in Petersfield. As well as other traditional garden features of the period, Petersfield Physic Garden contains a knot garden with over-and-under hedging, filled in with both plants and gravel.

CHAPTER SEVEN

HEALING GARDENS

The first healing gardens were planted in the Middle Ages by monks who practiced medicine with the herbs they grew. Later, in the sixteenth and seventeenth centuries, apothecaries and physicians planted physic gardens in which they grew plants for their medicinal properties. These were the first botanic gardens, designed to re-create the Garden of Eden by collecting together every known species of plant in the world.

RIGHT: According to the
doctrine of signatures, a
plant's visual characteristics
reveal in what way it can be
used medicinally.

n the earliest civilizations illness was thought to have been caused by the gods and could therefore only be treated by prayer, meditation, or exorcism. However, from around 2,000 B.C. people began to use plants to treat symptoms of illness, often alongside religious ritual. Plant medicine was practiced around the world, in China, Egypt, Africa, and North America.

ABOVE: In this manuscript of the Tractatus de Herbis by
Dioscorides, a woman is shown collecting honey for medicinal use.

The Greek physician and philosopher Aristotle, who lived in the fourth century B.C., adopted a less spiritual approach to plant medicine. He maintained that the body was made up of four humors — blood, phlegm, black bile, and yellow bile — reflecting the four elements of which the world was made — earth, air, fire, and water — and that these humors must be kept in equilibrium. Aristotle's contemporary, Theophrastus, listed over 550 species of plants that could be used medicinally to maintain this balance of humors within the body, and thereby maintain good health.

The Greek system of plant medicines influenced the Romans, whose most famous plant physician was Dioscorides, an army doctor, who lived in the first century A.D. He published a book, the *Tractatus de Herbis*, describing over 600 plants and their medicinal uses, and Dioscorides illustrated each plant himself from nature. Widely used across Europe, the book survived the fall of the Roman Empire and was still a standard work on the subject in medieval times.

In the Middle Ages it was the monks who mostly treated the sick, and they kept the art of gardening alive with their medicinal herb gardens. The herbs were often grown in narrow strip beds, often against the walls of the infirmary within the monastery. Sometimes healing gardens were grown in square plots, with raised beds in geometric formation.

MEN HERBAE MANDRAGORA

THE DOCTRINE OF SIGNATURES

It was traditionally believed that all plants displayed an indication of the illness they were created to treat. Pulmonaria has green leaves splashed with white dots. The leaves were thought to be the same shape as the lungs, and the dots resembled spittle, so the plant was used to treat diseases of the lungs. Its common names is lungwort. Lesser celandine has tiny tubers that resemble hemorrhoids, so it was used to treat piles. It is known as pilewort.

Sometimes the plant bore a more obscure similarity to the disease or illness it was believed to cure. For example, *Ophioglossum vulgatum*, or adder's tongue, was thought to be an effective treatment for snake bites since it resembled the tongue of an adder.

The color of flowers was another indication of their medicinal purpose. Red flowers were used to treat bleeding, from nose bleeds to serious hemorrhage, and plants with yellow flowers were used against jaundice and other liver diseases.

This approach to plant medicine, in which like treats like, was known as the Doctrine of Signatures, or the Doctrine of Similarities. Another approach popular at the time was astrological botany. Many classical gods and goddesses had been allocated specific plants with which they were associated. Once these classical gods had planets named after them, the plants were said to be ruled by those planets.

BELOW: The Garden of Eden was believed to contain every plant created, as well as the apple that caused Adam's fall.

Medicines from Paradise

The biblical references to the Garden of Eden had a huge impact on medicinal gardens. Since God had created all living plants as well as animals for the benefit of humans, it stood to reason that those that could not be eaten had some other function, the obvious explanation being that they were medicinal. It was already known that many plants had

therapeutic properties, so the assumption was that most other plants must also be able to cure illnesses and diseases.

The great explorers set out to discover the Garden of Eden, which was believed to contain every plant that had ever existed. But by the sixteenth century it was becoming plain that it wasn't there to be found. What had happened to it? The assumption was that it must have been broken up after Adam and Eve had been banished, in which case its contents would have been distributed around the world.

The first plant hunters aimed to travel around the globe collecting examples of every species in order to re-create Paradise. They brought these plants back from their travels and preserved them in botanical gardens, or physic gardens as they were often termed.

The idea was to study how these plants could be used medicinally for the benefit of humankind. Physic gardens were used by physicians as a source for medicines, and to investigate new treatments. Every plant collected by the explorers had to have a medicinal use if only it could be found. The gardens were also used for training students to ensure that they cured rather than killed their patients.

The earliest physic gardens were developed as part of the Italian Renaissance movement. The very first was planted in Pisa in 1543, followed by gardens in Padua and Florence.

The practice spread across Europe over the next century or so, until most major cities had their own physic garden. The first botanic garden in North America was planted outside Philadelphia in 1728 by an amateur Quaker doctor named John Bartram. He contributed to the European physic gardens by sending native American plants for their collections.

HERBALISM AND MEDICINE

There is an essential difference between the two closely related practices of herbalism and medicine. Herbalists believe that all illnesses and diseases can be treated with herbal remedies, an idea that has developed from the belief that plants were put on this Earth for our benefit. Medical doctors believe that plants have a use, but that many illnesses are better treated by mineral-based drugs.

Herbalists therefore use the whole plant to treat any particular illness; they traditionally believed – and still do – that all the constituents of the plant must work together in harmony to rebalance the body. Medical doctors, on the other hand, isolate individual chemicals when they use plants as a source for their drugs.

For many centuries, the herbalist's approach was the only one, and plants were grown to be administered as tinctures, infusions, or poultices of the whole plant. The plant was believed to treat not only the physical symptoms but also any mental, emotional, or spiritual ailments that were contributing to the illness.

THE COMPONENTS OF
THE HEALING GARDEN

Shape

There is no single layout typical to healing gardens, but there are certain designs that have been used frequently for centuries. The first of these is a square or rectangular garden, with regular small beds set within it. The solid shape of the square represents both human life and safety. Monastic gardens were often square – enclosing life – and the design of many healing gardens grew out of this tradition.

Circular gardens became popular from the 16th century. One of the first botanic gardens, at Padua, is laid out within a circular wall. The circle symbolizes infinity and perfection; it is a divine symbol. This made it suitable for use in botanic or physic gardens since the circle represents the eternal Paradise they were trying to emulate. Circular gardens are subdivided into smaller plots or beds, often arranged as a wheel around a central point to denote the Wheel of Life: both the changing seasons within the garden and the cycle of human life that the medicinal plants are there to help and ease in times of illness.

At the other extreme is the garden with no apparent design at all; the wild or cottage garden filled with healing plants. These were popular with wise women and ordinary people in the days when many people had no access to healing plants unless they grew them themselves. These gardens represent the wildness of nature, which is the source of these plants, and they imply a pagan overtone: it is nature who is giving her plants and flowers for the use of humankind.

Boundaries

The monastic gardens were walled, as we saw in an earlier chapter, to symbolize a haven of safety and peace; qualities that are especially valued in a healing garden. The early physic gardens were also walled. Since they were an attempt to re-create the Garden of Eden, containing every plant on Earth, they were enclosed in order to keep Paradise separate from the world. A solid boundary – rather than, for example, trellis – was necessary to keep the world out visually as well as physically.

Beds

Flower beds in physic gardens are almost always long and narrow. This is because narrow beds are easier to tend; you can reach everything without having to trample the plants. There is another reason, too: physic and botanic gardens were highly organized – often the flower beds were subdivided so that each plant had its own section, separated from its neighbors by a strip of boarding. If every plant in the world was to be collected and categorized for study, it was necessary to be very organized about the operation.

LEFT: Different varieties of a medicinal plant such as thyme make an ornamental feature when grown closely together.

ABOVE: Agrimonia eupatoria

(common agrimony)

ABOVE: Valeriana dioica *(left) (small marsh valerian) and* Valeriana officinalis *(great wild valerian)*

ABOVE: Origanum vulgare

(common marjoram)

Plants

There are literally thousands of plants with healing properties, and hundreds that have been grown and used for centuries. Some of these are well-known culinary herbs that also have medicinal uses, such as sage or garlic. Some are well-known garden flowers that can be used to cure wounds, ailments, or diseases; peony root, for example, was traditionally used as a sedative (although it is poisonous if taken in anything but very small quantities), and Madonna lily bulbs were used to ease skin conditions such as ulcers and burns.

Trees and shrubs also feature in healing gardens. Daphne bark or root is a traditional cure for ulcerous skin conditions; witch hazel is an astringent; myrtle used to be given as a treatment for bronchitis, and elder is given for fevers, coughs, colds, bronchitis; and as a laxative.

Many healing plants were grown for their associations with magic, or because they were thought to protect against evil, or drive out the devil. Traditionally this was as valid a reason for including a plant in a healing garden as the fact that it had valuable medicinal properties.

ABOVE: Matricaria camomilla

(wild camomile)

ABOVE: Alchemilla arvensis *(top) (parlsey piert) and* Alchemilla vulgaris *(common lady's mantle)*

ABOVE: Borago officinalis

(common borage)

St. John's wort, named because it was traditionally picked on St. John's Day (June 24th, also Midsummer's Day), was believed to drive away evil spirits because it was the flower of the sun, from which nothing could hide. Its association with Midsummer goes back to pagan times when it was the flower of the summer solstice. It is also a medicinal plant, which is effective for treating cuts, burns, and skin conditions, rheumatism, and stomach cramps.

Houseleek *(Sempervivum)* was grown to protect against fire; yarrow was used for divination both in the West and in China – the traditional Chinese system of divination, the *I Ching*, involved counting yarrow stalks to find the appropriate guidance. Daisies were thought to protect children from abduction by fairies; rosemary was believed to repel evil spirits; and vervain was used for purifying rituals, to remove hexes and curses, and for divination. Hellebore has long been grown to bring peace and calm to a troubled mind; especially to remove feelings of foreboding or unease. All of these were considered important aspects of healing, and healing gardens traditionally contained plants with a far wider range of uses than the purely medicinal.

Every Garden a Healing Garden

Although certain gardens have been tended traditionally for growing healing plants, there is of course a sense in which every true garden has the power to heal. The peacefulness and relaxation that a garden imparts has its own healing power to reduce stress and aid meditation. Perhaps this is why gardens have been treated as sacred places throughout history; simply because a garden seems to have as sacred and spiritual an influence as does a church or a temple.

ABOVE: Carum carvi *(caraway) is used for lack of appetite and as a digestive.*

RIGHT: A garden designed for the cultivation of healing plants can be balm to the senses. The healing garden can always accommodate informal flowering plants chosen for their cottage-garden looks rather than purely for their usefulness.

The kiss of the sun for pardon,
The song of the birds for mirth,
One is nearer God's heart in a garden
Than anywhere else on earth.

DOROTHY FRANCES GURNEY

BOTANIC GARDEN
PADUA, ITALY

This is a Renaissance botanic garden, one of the first of its kind in Europe. Although the plants in it have changed over the years, the design itself is as it was when it was first laid out in 1545. The design is contained within a circular wall, with the plot inside being subdivided into four quarters, with a pool in the middle. Each of the quarters is divided into four again, creating 16 areas in all. These areas would each have been planted with a different type of plant to help botanical students learn identification.

Two trees still survive in the garden at Padua since they were planted in 1550. One is the European fan palm *(Chamaerops humilis)*, and the other is the chaste tree *(Vitex agnuscastus)*.

MOUNT VERNON
OXFORDSHIRE, UK

The small garden of the Dr. Edward Bach Center contains many of the 38 flowers grown to make the range of Bach Flower Remedies, as well as many other garden flowers. Unlike the traditional physic gardens, such as those at Padua or Leiden, the garden is not laid out in an organized fashion but is a traditional cottage garden. This makes it a garden that is as relaxing and restful to the spirit as its flowers are to the mind when incorporated into the Flower Remedies.

UNIVERSITY OF OXFORD BOTANIC GARDEN
OXFORD, UK

This is the oldest botanic garden in Great Britain, having been established in 1621, when it was called the Oxford Physic Garden. It is in the center of Oxford, on the bank of the Cherwell River, and occupies just four and a half acres. It began as a collection of medicinal herbs for physicians in the seventeenth century and has evolved to become the most compact diverse plant collection in the world. It contains 8,000 species, representing almost every botanical family; there is nowhere else in the world where you can see such a variety of species in so little space.

Although many of these plants have been added since the garden was founded, it has evolved exactly in keeping with the intention of its founders: that it should contain every plant in the world in an attempt to re-create Eden. It is a beautiful walled garden to visit, but it is still used for its original purpose of education, hosting visits from schools, colleges, and other educational groups, and it is a research center for the study of the medicinal uses of plants.

THE WISE WOMAN'S GARDEN

The wise woman was traditionally an unofficial witch doctor of a village or location. She would be well versed in plant lore and would grow many healing plants in her own garden, as well as knowing where to collect others from local fields, woods, and hedgerows. People would visit to ask for a remedy for anything from warts to unrequited love, and she would give them charms and cures to help them.

Many people still continue this tradition and study plant lore in association with the traditional arts of astrology, and with charms and rituals. The garden is one of the most obvious places to observe the progress of the seasons as the flowers in it grow, die, and reappear the following year. The cycle of the year is also marked by the signs of the zodiac as they pass across the heavens. Since the planets rule astrological signs, the plants became associated with the signs. These plants are used to treat people born under the matching sign, or to treat the part of the body also governed by the same planet.

In 1645, Culpeper allocated herbs to each zodiac sign and recommended using these herbs to treat people born under the same sign with which the herb was associated. The wise woman's garden would often include a wheel-shaped herb garden divided into 12, each section containing the herbs associated with a different sign.

LEFT: The Roman goddess Flora, the goddess of flowers depicted on a fresco at Pompeii.

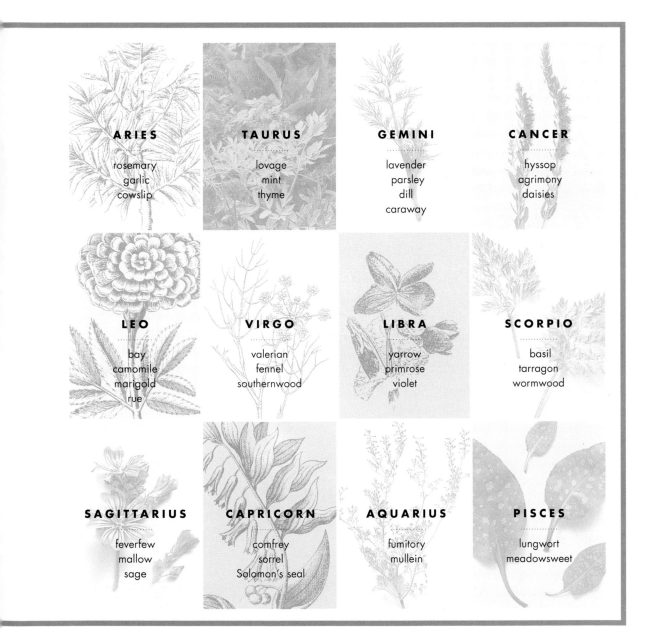

ARIES

rosemary
garlic
cowslip

TAURUS

lovage
mint
thyme

GEMINI

lavender
parsley
dill
caraway

CANCER

hyssop
agrimony
daisies

LEO

bay
camomile
marigold
rue

VIRGO

valerian
fennel
southernwood

LIBRA

yarrow
primrose
violet

SCORPIO

basil
tarragon
wormwood

SAGITTARIUS

feverfew
mallow
sage

CAPRICORN

comfrey
sorrel
Solomon's seal

AQUARIUS

fumitory
mullein

PISCES

lungwort
meadowsweet

ABOVE: Centaury is one of the plants used to make Bach flower remedies.

BELOW: Edward Bach discovered his flower remedies by studying the wild flowers growing in the countryside near his Oxfordshire home.

The Bach Flower Remedies

Edward Bach, a Harley Street doctor, was an expert in homeopathy. In the 1930s he preached the philosophy that a healthy mind led to a healthy body. He went on to draw up seven categories of emotions that could be treated homeopathically to create a positive outlook. These seven groups contained, among them, 38 negative states of mind. The Bach Flower Remedies were developed to treat these emotions. They were designed to stimulate the body's capacity to heal itself by balancing negative feelings and allowing the patient to take control.

Over the years these 38 remedies, which have been developed to be taken as drops in water to ease negativity, have become widely accepted and available. Dr. Bach made sure they were perfectly safe to use, even for children and pets. The 38 states of mind that they can treat, within the seven main categories of emotion, are as follows:

FEAR:
terror, fear of known things, fear of mind giving way, fears and worries of unknown origin, fear or over concern for others

LONELINESS:
pride and aloofness, impatience, self-centeredness

INSUFFICIENT INTEREST IN PRESENT CIRCUMSTANCES:
dreaminess, living in the past, resignation, apathy, lack of energy, unwanted thoughts and mental arguments, deep gloom with no origin, failure to learn from mistakes

DESPONDENCY OR DESPAIR:
lack of confidence, self-reproach and guilt, overwhelming feeling of responsibility, extreme mental anguish, after-effects of shock, resentment, exhaustion while struggling on, self-hatred

UNCERTAINTY:
seeking advice and confirmation of others, indecision, discouragement, hopelessness, "Monday morning" feeling, uncertainty about life

OVER-SENSITIVITY TO INFLUENCES AND IDEAS:
putting a brave face on mental torment, weak will and subservience, protectiveness about change and outside influences, hatred and jealousy

OVER-CARE FOR THE WELFARE OF OTHERS:
selfish possessiveness, over-enthusiasm, domineering inflexibility, intolerance, self-denial and self-repression

There is one other remedy, which Dr. Bach called "Rescue Remedy." It combines five flower remedies – rock rose, impatiens, clematis, star of Bethlehem, and cherry plum, for terror, impatience, dreaminess, the after-effects of shock, and fear of the mind giving way, respectively. The rescue remedy is used for coping with emotional trauma such as stage fright, visits to the dentist, or exams, as well as for administering to someone who is in shock.

Edward Bach lived and worked at a cottage in Oxfordshire called Mount Vernon. He collected many of the flowers he used from the surrounding countryside and made a garden at Mount Vernon that also contained many of the flowers used in his remedies. Mount Vernon is now the Dr. Edward Bach Center, where the mother tinctures for the remedies are still prepared using flowers from Dr. Bach's garden.

Dr. Bach believed that good health demanded a positive outlook on life and that God had provided all the plants that were needed to create such an attitude. He wrote:

Health is our heritage, our right. It is the complete and full union between soul, mind, and body; and this is no difficult far-away ideal to attain, but one so easy and natural that many of us have overlooked it.

CREATE YOUR OWN HEALING GARDEN

This design is for a healing garden in a pattern that symbolizes everything in the universe. At its center is a cross, for humanity; the vertical line symbolizes masculinity and the horizontal line femininity. A cross within a circle is also a symbol of the changing seasons of the year. The circle itself represents Heaven, and the square around it symbolizes the Earth.

The four triangular beds in the corners each contain a different-colored herb representing the four elements — earth, air, fire, and water — from which everything else derives. The medicinal plants in the eight beds are divided according to the type of ailments they treat. The pool of water creates a center of calm stillness in the garden. This could be the layout for a small garden, or part of a larger one.

KEY

1. Brick paths
2. Yellow and orange nasturtiums, representing earth
3. Catmint (blue) representing air
4. Red-leaved basil representing fire
5. Lady's mantle (green) representing water

PLANTS TO REDUCE STOMACH UPSETS:
6. Marjoram
7. Peppermint
8. Green basil

PLANTS TO HELP THE DIGESTION:
9. Coriander
10. Fennel
11. Sweet Cicely
12. Dill

PLANTS TO SOOTHE SKIN COMPLAINTS:
13. Comfrey
14. Mint
15. Mullein

PLANTS TO HEAL WOUNDS:
16. Garlic
17. Golden rod
18. Bistort
19. Hyssop

PLANTS TO EASE HEADACHES:
20. Feverfew
21. Lavender
22. Rosemary

PLANTS TO TAKE AS A TONIC:
23. Costmary
24. Parsley
25. Salad burnet
26. Yarrow

PLANTS TO ENCOURAGE SLEEP:
27. Camomile
28. Valerian
29. Lemon verbena

PLANTS TO REDUCE FEVERS:
30. Marigold
31. Sage
32. Chervil
33. Lemon balm

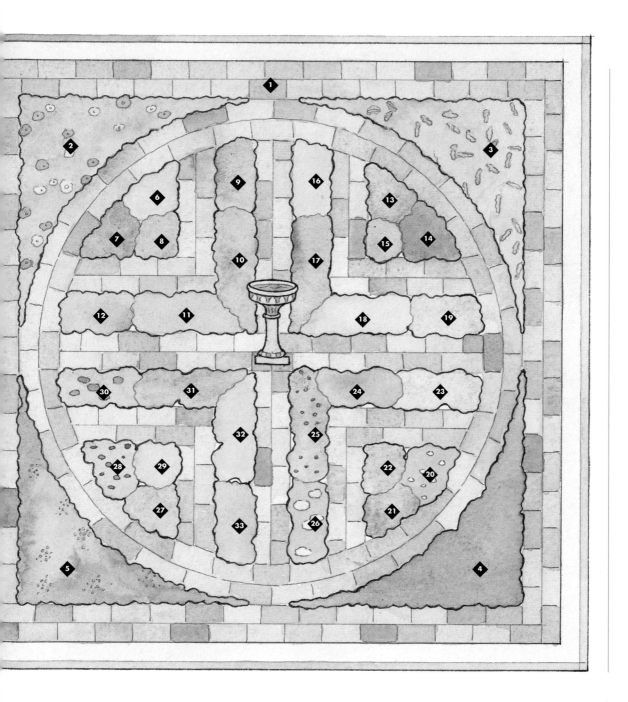

THE CHALICE WELL GARDEN
GLASTONBURY, SOMERSET, UK

This is a very different kind of healing garden from the physic gardens; it contains a healing spring that flows through the garden. Glastonbury is associated with the legend of King Arthur; it is also said to have been visited by Joseph of Arimathea accompanied by the child Jesus. The town is built around the ruins of a medieval abbey, and the town and its Tor – a hill that rises sharply from the plains around it – has long been a place of pilgrimage.

The spring water has a high iron content, which may account for its healing properties. It fills a well at one end of the garden and then runs over a waterfall into the next section of the garden, known as King Arthur's Court. Here, it fills the Pilgrim's Bath, where many people are said to have been healed.

The whole of the garden is laid out to create an atmosphere that heals the mind and the spirit as well as the body; it is beautifully planted with flowers and trees, and visitors are asked to respect certain areas set aside for meditation.

LEIDEN BOTANIC GARDEN
LEIDEN, HOLLAND

The original physic garden at Leiden was created in 1587 by Carolus Clusius; the garden open to the public today is a painstaking re-creation of the original. Clusius was responsible for launching the Dutch passion for tulips when his own collection, brought from Vienna, began to produce unusual color variations such as stripes or splashes of a second color. His botanic garden was divided into four quarters, each of which was subdivided into two sections containing narrow strip beds in which different plant species were categorized. The garden, now called the "Hortus Clusianus," is surrounded by buildings and has been re-created with trelliswork, which featured in the original garden, raised beds, and archways.

FURTHER READING

The Principles of Gardening
Hugh Johnson
MITCHELL BEAZLEY 1979

Plants in Garden History
Penelope Hobhouse
PAVILION BOOKS 1992

The Quest for Paradise
Ronald King
WHITTET WINDWARD 1979

In the Japanese Garden
Michael S. Yamashita & Elizabeth Bibb
CASSELL 1995

The Healing Garden
Sue Minter
HEADLINE 1994

The Garden of Eden
John Prest
YALE UNIVERSITY PRESS 1981

Restoring Period Gardens
John Harvey
SHIRE PUBLICATIONS 1988

The Garden – Visions of Paradise
Gabrielle van Zuylen
THAMES AND HUDSON 1995

The Medieval Garden
Sylvia Landsberg
BRITISH MUSEUM PRESS

Plants from the Past
David Stuart & James Sutherland
PENGUIN BOOKS 1989

Oriental Gardens
Norah Titley & Frances Wood
THE BRITISH LIBRARY 1991

INDEX

ACKNOWLEDGEMENTS

A-Z Botanical Collection: Johnston 104/5; Cooper 106; Wheeler 107; Chandler 109; Chandler 110/1; Tyrey 118/9

Ancient Art & Architecture Collection: 46/7

Bridgeman Art Library: Timothy Easton 6; BL Add Ms 105 46f29r; British Library 61; Kunstinstitut, Frankfurt 72; Bib. Nat, Vienna 74; British Library 76/7; Gemaldegalerie, Kunstintitut Vienna 124

Chalice Well Garden, Glastonbury: 138

e t archive: 39; Musee de Cluny 78; 86/7; 97; 98; Bib. Estense, Moderna 122 & 125; Archeological Museum, Naples 132; 139

Mary Evans Picture Library: 9

Futile Press Collection: 51; 53; 75; 90/91

Glasgow Museums Service, St Mungo's Cathedral: 8

Robert Harding Picture Library: Front cover, Watts; 14; 30; Inverni 44/5; 58/9; Rawlings 91; Newton 92/3; Newton 99; Proud 102; Watts 129

Hutchison Picture Library: 15 ; Pemberton 16; Page 18/19; 21; Pemberton 22; Goycolea 31 & 33; McIntyre 34/5; McIntyre 38; 48; Goycolea 49; Francis 52; Tree 57; Souter 60; Francis 64; 65

ImageBank: Yuan Hao Ma 12/13; Alcosser 80/81

Images; 32; 40; 120/1

Images of India: 54

Joe Low: 115

Oxford Botanical Garden; Timothy Walker: 130/1

The Shrewsbury Quest: 66/7; 84/5

Spectrum Colour Library: 112

Elizabeth Whiting Associates: 126; 134b

Zefa: Front cover; 17; Orion 28/9; 36/7; 88/9; 103; 128

All other images from the BRIDGEWATER BOOK COMPANY Collection